MW01229665

1

Going Through to Let It Go

A story of erasing life's trauma through metaphysical

strategies and philosophies.

By

Dr. Zelda Hayes

Edited by: *Pamela R. Shomo*

Contents

PREFACE

Laughing out loud at how many years of therapy had no real results, I took my life into my own hands and went to my inner self, my ancestors, and my creator and after thirty days of real meditation and self-evaluation, I discovered some deep shit. I picked up the phone and call my counselor and when he asked when I would like to schedule our next session, as he didn't want me to linger too far past the thirty days I missed, I informed him, I no longer needed his services. He actually tried to argue this with me by stating to stopping so abruptly could cause more damage than good. I explain to him I found the solutions to my situation given straight from a higher source. He asked me what my source was, and I replied, "my higher consciousness." I could hear his irritation through his persistence and ridicule. I simply told him, I got this. "No, you don't he replied" My reply was "Fuck your couch" and I hung up the phone. Let me begin by saying in no way is my goal here to degrade the psychological profession or its methods. What my intention here in writing fuck your couch, is to analyze my life, on a spiritual level since this cognitive stuff is only a portion of the acknowledgment. What I discovered was for every physical alignment, behind it is a spiritual unbalance. Believing it or not, doesn't make it not so. I found several "powerful action steps "that had I done would have saved me a lot of pain. I decided I would start doing those powerful action steps while I am alive.

Now over twenty years later I am still doing it and I tell you this. Although I started with no money, no friends, and no love I made it. The journey was long and painful, yet I am God's greatest masterpiece and I know that now and every day I make sure my life reflects that which I am. This my sister is what I want to share with you. You are also God's greatest masterpiece, and to avoid sounding like I am male-bashing, I will say this, they don't want you to know "how to activate your power."

One of the questions I used to ask, and I am sure you ask it too, was, "what is my purpose?" The answer is simply this in my opinion" Create your own legacy and enjoy the experience until the next birth. Wherever that birth may be. Over the next several chapters, I will share with you first, my life story and the lessons learned, then I will share with you the action steps that equipped me with activating my own power so that I could enjoy this life experience granted me by the Creator, that which we call God.

My mission is more than sharing my story, but to help you

activate your power and connect to higher consciousness without fear as well. I will not be as pleasant in some parts. It may even sound as if I am being harsh with you. Make no mistake my friend, I am. It's sugarcoating your life, which got you here. Playtime is officially over.

As you read my story, you will find yourself seeing yourself in pain, I write. You will recognize women you know who went through the same struggle. With that being said, understand that at no fault of our own, our culture being enslaved took away our right to be crowned as the Queens we are. The duties, roles, and rights of a Queen must now be earned through growth as opposed to a crowning ceremony. While many of us have taken on this title by mere right, it is unfair to call yourself as such if you have not gone through some sort of growing process. As you read, my crazy life, you will see how it consisted of many violations, neglect, and heartbreak. My attempted suicide was my breakthrough in recognition of not only who I was but what I was. I now invite you to turn your pain into power and do your own crowning as your life was the actual ceremony. You survived; initiation is complete. Now, design your own crown and wear it proudly in all that you do. Embrace the truth that there is power after pain if you are paying attention and put in the work to be your own co-creator. Make your enemies bow down to you.

Not physically, but emotionally, financially, and with the authority of the true level of respect you deserve.

Yes, I attempted to indulge in therapy, and it helped, but just a little. What was left out was the most important thing I needed, especially as a black woman. Traditional therapy did not help me find my spiritual strength, which I found later on in life was the answer to all the issues I was dealing with. Traditional therapy did allow me to hide my pain by pumping me with pills to make me feel good. However, after they wore off, the pain came back, and I found myself keeping those pills on my bedside to avoid having to experience any minute of pain, anxiety, depression, or hallucinations.

Years of practicing meditation would soon show me that I was not hallucinating but actually had a spiritual gift, that my third eye was open, that I had ancestors trying to connect with me. I would have to get off those happy pills, which also, by the way, were affecting other areas of my body. I was being broken down and recreated into a zombie with no feelings of giving a dam. I was no longer a patient; I was a customer.

My external freedom did not begin until a year after I moved to Florida and have decided to put the past me. I started with the following steps of initiation by healing myself. For only through healing can you see your true self. When you see your true self and accept it, the world will also. Otherwise, if you don't know who you are, the world will tell you, you will believe it, and lack of self is a great sin. My healing process began with defining myself, which was to accept the fact that I was a Black Queen, and I would have to start walking a Black Queens walk, talk a Black Queens talk and demand my due from life by using the gifts already within me. Giving no thought to yesterday.

Before I go into the grimy details of my life, let me first warn you that what you are about to read is all true, except for the parts that are not, with a few changes in names to protect those I mention. This story is a reader's discretion is advised for nothing about the life I lived at was pretty or clean, to say the least. The ugliness I endured was not a test of God or the complete fault of my parents, but more to do with the fact that being born gifted with the discernment of spirits, yet never heading to the warnings I was presented with played a lot to do with the events that I am about to unfold before you. Let the record show my truth that not only did I temporarily hate God for the life I lived, but I also secretly hated the fact that he or she, for that matter, instructed me to write this book for empowering you and instilling hope into your minds and hearts. I felt wasn't life painful enough then to have my dark secrets and humiliation exposed. I remember when I was around nine or ten walking to the alter on a rainy Sunday with the woman who raised me, and to this day, I called her mom.

The Usher had asked me, "What is it you want from God?" My age was young yet, my mind was old, as I replied," I want God to make me a good girl and use me to make other girls good too." I'm not sure if even then I knew what that meant. Yet standing there on my terrace with that gun to my head, I think back now and wonder if I didn't get what I asked for. As an adult today, I now know what being "used" by God means, and its' not pretty. It's being taken through the mud, and if you can hold on long enough, coming out as bright as diamonds. More importantly, I believe I was instructed to demonstrate the power of the subconscious, which is the voice of God. It was this voice that I have heard, which you have heard, and perhaps because we've not been taught the true value of it, ignored it, and went with the voice of the ego or our conscious thought when I made choices.

The reason I feel the need to explain this at the beginning of this book is so that you will be aware of its existence and be able to point out when those voices were shaping in my life and as you see yourself through my pain, will be able to take with you its' process and perhaps avoid any more pain in your life from that moment on. To demonstrate that we have a responsibility to hold ourselves accountable, not always for the choices we made, but how we have allowed it to make us feel in the present moment. Pain has no purpose in our present. So now, my sisters, read, embrace, learn, and take it all in, my life and the lessons written therein, that you may find peace within your storm and begin the healing process. This book is for you, for your healing, for the breaking of conditioned minds and all so-called generational curses. Yet no this, no matter how grim the story, nor how filthy I may appear during my process, should you find your twin in this book, don't beat yourself up with guilt, for we have all done things for us on personal reasons or way of healing, but forgive yourself first, and if it gets too intense and you feel as if that dark side of yourself pushes your thoughts toward   ending it all, do as I did when I woke up to the voice of life and utter aloud to yourself, "I am not a mess, I am a masterpiece."

INTRODUCTION

It was only ten a.m. in the morning: the sun had already made its way on the city of New York. A warm breeze filled the air, blanketing me as if to say, "it's ok, girl."

But I had disregarded that message as I stood on the balcony of my twelve-story apartment in Lefrak City, Queens. I was looking down with envy at the people moving about, most likely on their way to work. Dressed for success, I could even hear the laughter that came from small crowds that stood below. "Must be nice to laugh," I thought to myself. However, laughter was no longer a luxury in my life. Wiping my tears, I began to feel a bit dizzy.

I didn't realize that I had drunk over a half bottle of vodka. I no longer cared anymore. "These men always tell you they love you; they don't love me! They just want me for what lays between my legs! Isn't that the right world? You could give two shits if I jumped," I screamed

aloud.

"Yeah, that's what I thought; I hate you, God! You played me, and you played me! Just like everyone else. You said you loved me, and that joy would come in the morning.

Where's my joy? My words were trembling like my body, which is by now sweaty and dirty from crying for the last three hours. Tired and mentally exhausted from the hell that seemed to find me in this life without an ounce of mercy and to add insult to injury, today I was facing eviction by five o clock, this home I worked so hard to build. The only thing working utility in my apartment for the last thirty days was my telephone, and I had to lie on my back to get that bill paid; however, this would be the one time I would not answer it as it began to ring. How did I get here, to this place of desperation? Where death seemed to be the only way for me to be free from this current pain.

I believed God owed me a different life other than this one. I would not wait until he decided when I would die; hell, he decided everything else, and it was not working for me. Lifting the .38 caliber from the coffee table, I loaded one bullet and

put it to my temple; I cursed God "and pulled the trigger. Problem solved!

MISS MY DADDY

I can honestly say that while I have heard from so many people how cute I was as a child or bright or gifted they said I was, I have never felt any of those things. So, I was high yellow or, as they call us today, redbone. So, my hair was so soft and long that you could not put it into an afro, or when it got wet, I was automatically the perfect poster kid for the Jeri curl. Did that define me? Worst of all, I have never felt loved. At least not the kind of love that I was yearning. I was yearning for a love that made me feel safe at night, unique in the day, and valid all year long. A feeling that said I mattered to someone simply because I existed, not because of what I looked like outside.

On the outside, beauty may exist, but inside I was a mess, and I knew it, even as a little girl.

This love is the love most are supposed to receive from their parents.

I understand now being an adult; my birth mother had many demons to deal with; she had been a victim of so many things that her parental duties were overlooked in her quest for love. Slowly as I grew up, my mother had my forgiveness because I too eventually carried those same types of demons. I hold more anger towards my father for not helping her heal and becoming another cross she would have to bear. In that began my suffering. I found it hard to forgive a man who could leave a woman with a child, have children spread over the place, and not provide for them. My father was already married when he met mom, yet with all she was going through, he still managed to utter the words that if God can forgive him, the heck what anyone thinks of him. Well, dad, I am not God, and I cannot forgive you as quickly. I cannot call him anything less than an irresponsible whore who found God when he got old sadly believed that if God forgives him, the hell with how his children felt. So now I get to grow up becoming an additional burden in addition to the two my mother already had, making me hate men with a passion. It is through actions like this that women today acquire the "Daddy issue" that Already taught us to not trust a man by how our mothers are treated. Or even worse, that we were not significant enough to stay. The sad part is that because we're not shown anything else (most of the time), we end up with those trust issues embedded in us.

I met my father during my first-grade graduation; he showed up out of nowhere in an orange punch boxcar. My mother said,' This is your father" Because I was a child, I was filled with so much excitement. "I do have a father, I thought to myself." I was so overwhelmed at the thought that I hadn't realized he hadn't even hugged me or said hello. They just looked at me, opened the door for me to get into the car, closed it, and began conversing with my mother. Thoughts of happily ever after, nonetheless, still pondered in my head. "No more teasing from the neighborhood kids of being without a dad," I thought to myself.

He will make sure mom has food and lessen those hungry nights of not having enough. Perhaps even get me my bed so all five of us will no longer have to sleep on that pull-out couch. Life began to look wondrous in my eyes.

God was finally answering the prayers of his child. There I sat, giggling in the back seat as my mind entertained a new life as a real family. He came to my graduation, and I could no longer remember the words to the song as my class performed. I was too busy making plans. After the ceremony was over, we all headed back to the car.

"Can I sit upfront with you, daddy"? "Ok, get in," he said. It did not dawn on me how silent the ride going back was, as I was still entertaining what my new life would be like. We arrived at my grandmother's house instead of my home. I jumped out of the car, still in excitement, a smile on my face.

Then in the blink of an eye, I watched my mother get out of the car, and my dad drove off like a bad guy running from the cops. He did not even say goodbye. My eyes filled with tears as I was filled with a child's confusion. Not understanding what just happened, did I do something wrong? I asked myself. This pain I was feeling was physically making my chest hurt, and I could not move; I felt like my whole world had just ended. I understand today that this is what abandonment feels like. I was not too fond of it.

What my father left behind was an imprint of hate and pain, and confusion that would follow me for the rest of my life. As I grew, I began to blame myself during a breakup; I would seek high and low to find a man that would give me that security of love and safety I was seeking from my father. It also created a spirit of revenge in my heart that prayed for my father to burn into flames in the presence of my mother, and she would be vindicated for her pain, the one he added to. Yes, he would pay for every pain my mother felt from that moment on.

Growing up R&B hits defined me to the letter. "Annie Mae," people are saying I was growing up too fast. Need they ask why? I was born in 1966, not the most excellent era for a black woman, especially if she was single with four children with different fathers. To this day, I don't see how men find it ok to increase an army of baby mamas instead of wives. Dana: was the oldest, then Cynthia, the middle sister who sang like an angel and received plenty of attention from a family who loved to put her in the center of the room at family gatherings to sing since she was eight years old. My younger brother Brice stayed to himself most of the time, and lastly, there was me.

Planted by a man who had already deposited so many other seeds elsewhere, I was already part of a tribe before birth. As she carried me, I had already labeled a burden, a thorn in her side.

This I confirm with the name she gave me.

My mother decided to name me "Zelda" ironically, my name was a nickname for the feminine name Griselda, which may originally have meant "dark battle," and the feminine form of the Yiddish name Selig, meaning "blessed," "happy." already defined me in the womb, and my life would be both definitions.

I know that God doesn't make any mistakes; thus, I make no apologies for being who I am. All I did was breathe. Perhaps the labeling came from the knowledge of who my parents were.

At eight years old, I knew nothing of relationships to judge right and wrongs. Yet, through the eyes of a child, if all the other kids in the neighborhood had a man in the house,

I felt so should ours, and wherever our fathers were, it was my secret prayer that they would magically burn while they were alive, and my mother would see this, and she would be vindicated for her sorrow.

I always did things my way, never entertained the rules.
Never saw the point.

Some would say I was too much to be in this
world, yet still, here I am. Some say that since I am an accident, I
would cause more havoc than peace. She is too active, too
outspoken, too fast, too strong-willed. She thinks too highly of
herself and asks excessively many questions. She will be your
burden. Ironically, they were all right. I am still to this day all
those things with a touch of arrogance that sways when I move. I
dance to no one's tune. However, these traits were bestowed upon
me while I was in my mother's womb. Thus, they are mine by
default. A choice that was chosen for me without my consent.
Little did I know these traits would be needed for my survival.

I don't know what it was about me that triggered my
hands to always be on my hips, flat-chested. Yet, I still managed
to keep them poked out, playing with my hair when I spoke in a
manner unbecoming of a girl my age, Long red hair too curly to
style and too straight to put in an afro even if you blew it out with
a blow dryer, skin so light I was constantly called a yellow heifer,
a beautiful smile, and a body that the sun could borrow energy
from.

A sinful skill that falls upon the spirit of little girls and women alike, all because of neglect, intentional or not. This was my curse. My body thought it had all the answers, but my spirit disagreed. However, my spirit would often leave me hanging when I made a wrong turn; it would never jump in and stop me until it was too late. I have always walked on my toes, a congenital disability that still plagues me; however, this gave me the perception of being taller with longer legs and the perfect curve in my calves. Legs that made grown men with wives turn their heads. I must be honest and say that I enjoyed all the attention from these so-called uncles and aunties. (My mother's friends) Where did I get this behavior?

Was it something I saw on television? Something I had seen the adults do. Oh no, I know what it was. I got the looks from the men and women within my environment. It made me feel special like I mattered. They saw me, they loved me, they cared about me.

They never touched me, at least not with their hands. Yet it was at this stage I learned that the mind was a tool that could be used powerfully. I learned that a look said more than a word, and a sexy swerve could be a whole paragraph. I never realized that the look I was giving was so seductive until I noticed the erections that grew on the men I was looking at. I could make a man erect, and a woman's nipples stand tall with little to no effort.

In the back of my mind, I knew this was a dangerous game, but hell, as young as I was and as old as they were, they should not have entertained it in the first place. Throwing all those compliments to a child, you all know the ones. You are going to be a heartbreaker when you grow up. Look at you, filling out like a woman! Sit on auntie's lap. Remember, if you need anything, anything at all, you call me, and I will get it for you.

Holding me way too close, stroking my back and neck, playing in my hair, and feeling her breast way too close to me, I didn't know if I should push her away or hug her back and pull her closer. After all, when a child feels unwanted, ignored, and unloved, they will allow pretty much allow anyone to move in close to them—the basic need for affection, which is my excuse. As I look back today, I wonder just how many women learned this look like a child to gain the basic needs of life....Love.

If you think about it, women were placed into positions from childhood to use their bodies as tools for affection as parents were out trying to gain love and forgot those children. Emotional needs were not met, so what does one do? Utilize instincts of attraction that to this day some call a jezebel. After endless teasing from my peers, I realized that my mother was bi-sexual; thus, I had endless aunts and uncles to use my new talent. To this day, I always ask myself why I was singled out. What was it about me that made them single me out? My siblings were taken care of by the family, but somehow, I was the one who would be helped, but with restrictions.

You can stay this day, but not that; you cannot have a key, etc. I came to the sad conclusion that I was on my own, and my family did not seem to have a problem with me being left behind.

I was the strong one, always able to bounce back to the family. What kind of bullshit burden was that to lay on a fourteen-year-old?

A burden that I would carry on my shoulders for the rest of my life, and no one was there to help remove the weight. Every family has at least one Medea mother figure, if not two. Well, as God would have it, I had a Medea that introduced me to God when things were getting crazy at home somehow.

(And I still don't know to this day) I ended up with my sisters Dana's aunt Mrs. Karen Porter. She was Dana's Father's family member. Who willingly played the role of my mother? I can only recall visiting Mrs. Porter with my sister, next thing I knew, Dana was going back home, and I was told I was staying. Since this was a household with a family setting and plenty of food, they got no rebuttal from me.

Mrs. Porter was a Godly woman, married with two sons, older than I. The mom who paid attention to me, the mom who taught me how to sew, cook, clean, garden, etc.

It was not long before my sister's aunt Karen became a mom and Uncle Darren willingly became a daddy. It was beautiful for a while as she would take me to church. I joined the choir and threw myself at the altar, spoke in tongues, and was sure God was here now and forever to see me through this life. Then for reasons unknown, my biological mother ordered me back home. Then the drama of excessive grown-ups in and out of my house began with little food and instability. Again. One day, I remember seeing my mother kiss one of my make-believe aunts, and that moment caused me great sexual confusion.

This new craft of seduction got me through my junior high school years. It came to me naturally—the ability to give a look that spoke louder than words. Shoulders back and chest out, head high. Never thump when you walk, sway like a soft spring breeze. That's a lady. That's what I was forcing myself to become, way too soon. Yet only because I was seeking that real love. Then one day, as my sister and I were walking, something new took place. We were both confronted by a very sexy young man (who had no idea I was only fourteen). "Hey, girls," a deep voice, smooth swag, and broad shoulders. As fast as lighting, feeling as if I must be the winner of this moment (since my sister got enough attention from everyone else in my mind) in my fastest turn, hands-on-hips," you talking to me"? "I am talking to the both of you," he replied, this grown man who was no taller than I was.

His complexion was like a Hershey's milk chocolate bar, his chest broader than the young boys my age on the block. His body was built like a God in my mind. There was no reason for me to look below his waist, yet I was curious to see if he was erect.

Why I do not know.

At that moment, I realized the members come in various sizes, and though I was still a virgin, I was impressed with the large bulk I noticed in the front of his pants, demonstrating he was defiantly packing. "Well, my name is Zelda," I replied in a tone that said it would be in your best interest to know me. "What is your name"? I acted as if my sister was not even there. She gets enough attention running away and having our family send me to find her.

It's my time to get a bit of love. "I'm Troy," he said, "are you coming back" outside?

"Would you like me to"? I stated in my most sensual voice.

"Oh, most definitely."

"So, tell me, Troy, if I come back out, what do you have in store for me? I would hate to think I am wasting my time." (Boy, did I have the game lined up, I thought to myself)

However, so did Troy, as his reply was, "Tell me what I should have, and I will see if it can be done."

"I want a conversation with substance."

Damn! I was deep. Yet, it made no sense to waste my time if it would not lead to something worth being bothered by. As it turned out, Troy was worth coming back outside for, and as for my sister, she never thought twice about him. As it also turned out, although Troy was short, he was 21 years old! I did not find this out until about a week of dating him. There was no need for me to ask as I figured it; he is the same height; he must be the same age. That is what happens when a child uses childlike logic.

We had an intense conversation for the first few weeks; I was introduced to Louis Farrakhan at a lecture. At first, I thought this was deep. Knowing so much about my blackness and what games the white man was playing on me. However, after a while, it got old. I felt no black or white man is responsible for my life. I am. No one can stop me unless I let them.

Therefore, I decided it was time to stop venturing my knowledge for the sake of black power. The only power I ever needed was God's power.

I did, however, enjoy the many lessons of foreplay with Troy. I mastered it with ease. Yet I would never let him penetrate out of fear of going to hell since I was not married to him. My creativity never slept. One night I decided that Troy earned enough points and trust to see a little more of my flesh and relieve himself without being inside of me. It was a warm spring evening when Troy and I went out to dinner at my favorite restaurant on Fordham Road. It was crowded being a Friday, but I had the night planned and was not concerned about the time.

The waiter came and escorted us to our table. He sat us at a nice cozy booth, not too close to the kitchen or restrooms. We ordered our meals and entertained each other with small talk until our food arrived. Then when the waiter placed our meals in their proper place, I quickly put my thoughts out there at Troy to see how fast he could catch it.

"Troy, would you like to go to a hotel after dinner"? Troy almost choked on his food. His eyebrows showed the excitement of a child on Christmas morning. (Rubbing his hands together in excitement) 'Are you sure he asked"? (My head tilted slightly to the side by way of appearing seductive, with my eyes speaking for me) I would not bring it up if I were not, was my reply. 'Well, you know if we go, there will be no dry humping going on; we can do that at my house."   We both laughed. I laughed a

26

little harder at the thought of what I had in mind.

    We arrived at the hotel about an hour after the suggestion. We walked into the room; it was your average hotel room, nothing special. Floral tapestry on the walls and beige comforters, a large picture of a strange abstract portrait of pastel colors, gives it a soft flare. I dimmed the lights immediately and let out a sigh that turned me on. Troy was out of his shirt before I could say a word. I had to move fast; this was not what he thought. I would initiate, keeping the ball in my court, giving me all power that night. I walked over to him and began to undo his pants; when I got to his ankles, I motioned him to lie down. I reached over to the clock radio and turned on my favorite station, 107.1 WBLS. There was a lover's serenade of love songs on Friday nights until 11 p.m. I stood in front of the bed and slowly began to undress. Enjoying the view of his penis rising, and I had not even touched him yet. Kissing his legs and purposely allowing my hair, which was a perfect long length back then, glide across his legs and thighs.

    I gently kissed his member and immediately heard him sighing in excitement. I lay on top of him, still wearing my black bra and no panties. (Only because I wasn't wearing any, never liked them) I purposely placed my breast upon his chest and began kissing him with long, deep hot passionate kisses. He attempted to grab hold of his penis for entry, but that was not on the menu. In my mind, if I did not have sex, I still had a chance to go to heaven. No ring, no kitty, just play with it, but no entry. That was my motto.

I took my hands, held both his hands, and locked them into mine, and while using my thighs, I cupped his member between them and began to stroke slowly and tightly. The illusion of being inside of a hot tight, and warm pussy without being inside at all. I was a creative young woman. At first, he had a look that said, what are you doing? But quickly after that, he was amazed and stunned.

His moaning said he was enjoying the ride I was delivering. My hips move back and forth, then circle motions with a few fast-thrusting gestures, and then back to slow. I was being turned on myself as I felt him stroking against my clitoris.

I lifted my head and began to make eye contact, and shortly after that, Troy began to suck extremely hard on my neck as he began to explode all over the both of us. My plan worked perfectly, and I did not have to lose my virginity. Now we could continue our relationship without the pressure of intercourse.

From the words of Janet Jackson, it was time for me to take control. We would date and be intimate but on my terms. Months went by, and nothing changed too much; my sister Cynthia began running away often when my mother got on her nerves. I was being sent to go and find her. Back. My little brother Brice was sent to live with my cousin, and eventually, my older sister Dana was smart enough to get married and get the hell out of the house. Finally, Cynthia left at home ran away for good this time.

She did not want to be found. In all my heart, I don't blame her. My mother's pain was evident through how my sister was treated.

I could only pray that wherever she was, God would keep her in his care. I later learned that she was living with our grandmother. Hell, I want to stay too. I asked grandma if I could stay, she smiled at me and told me I would be fine, to stay with my mother. That was a blow to my heart that my grandmother didn't even want me. That is fine; I convinced myself.

Troy loves me, and that is enough.

Countless fights from the neighborhood kids stopped since I was now wearing name-brand clothes and was sharper than they were. However, life took another blow when I came home from school. "Zelda, come here" her voice was stern and frightening. "Yes," I replied. "Are you having sex with that boy?" "Of course not!" This was an insult to me. "Mama Karen already told me I have to be married, so I don't need your advice" "Dear Lord" did I just say that aloud?' Before I could take it back and say sorry, my face swung hard to the left side of my body, leaving behind a fiery feeling as if to warn me what hell feels like. Me and my sassy mouth. I can only laugh at it now; I have never learned to speak with diplomacy. My mother went into my room and packed up everything Troy bought me, which was everything I ever owned. No-fault of her own; after all, she was doing it all by herself. I understand that now.

"Let's go," she said. The next thing I knew, I was at the door of Troy's home. Whom he shared with his mother. This is so humiliating; what is she doing? I thought to myself. She looked at me hard as she knocked on their door. Here you go. If you want to date her, you take care of her.

Everybody's jaws especially mind, hit the floor. Then she turned and walked away. She eventually moved to where I don't know. Did she just drop me off like yesterday's trash?

Hold your tears in, don't you dare cry, I thought to myself. "I am not going to question the sanity of a woman who drops her child off to a grown man's house." Shaking her head, Troy's mother, Ms. Sharon, motioned me to enter. "You will sleep in here with me. You are not to distract my son from his studies." Studies? I did not know Troy was in college. I did not even know he was an architect; I was already impressed. I could have quickly gone back to Ms. Porter's house, but this was more fun.

I get to play wife, and maybe he will marry me, I would think to myself as every child does when young and allegedly in love. After a while playing wife as a fifteen-year-old gets old, I want to go outside and play; instead, I'm here making dinner. This new life, 1982, the error of big hair, lacy gloves, and the sounds of independence from Janet Jackson and Jimmy Jam. Every girl wanted to be like her. 'What have you done for me" was a hit, but I couldn't relate to it since Troy took outstanding care of me. Yet, he became more and more like a brother than a lover.

Now I could relate to the song "Control," as that was what I was seeking. To somehow take control of my life and a life of stability and genuine love. Whatever that was.
Blasting my cassette player and grooving, I began ironing Troy's clothes while he and his mom were out working. "I'm in control" yeah, it was time for a change, but I did not know how it was going to come about. I had too much freedom and no discipline—another dangerous element for a young girl's life. In my heart, I was ready to trade in my childish treasures and step into womanhood. A prevailing thought, I am sure, when it comes to today's girls. My sisters, I stop briefly to tell you this. You may very well be in pain but take it from my experience and believe me when I tell you, your daughters feel double your pain even more because they don't understand. So, guard them with your life and let your presence be

"felt."

I changed the cassette and began to listen to Stacy Lattisaw's "Let Me Be Your Angel. I was ready to give Troy all of me. I wanted to be his wife, and I assumed that having sex with him would make him want to marry me. I wanted to mean something to someone, anyone, and I felt so very insignificant. I felt as if I was just here in this world, without purpose. I believed that if I gave up my virginity to Troy, it would fill the emptiness.

Like most girls, I believed that the first night would be as you watch television. Romantic, sweet, and passionate. I realized that television lies and nothing on it was real. That night when Troy came in, I greeted him at the door, and when I hugged him, I whispered in his ear, I am ready for you to make me a woman. He smiled, looked me in my eyes, and said, I will take care of you. I did not know what that meant, so I disregarded it and hugged him again. Troy took me to his cousin's home; he had the key. He opened the door and looked at me, saying, "don't worry, he won't be back till tomorrow. Troy led me to the back bedroom. I suddenly felt terrified, I did not know what to expect, and the unknown was something I never liked. Turning on the soft lamp, Troy lite incense, turned and popped in a cassette into the player.

The sounds of Earth Wind & Fire singing "reasons" filled the room. My body was trembling so hard I could not make it stop. Seeing that I was frightened, Troy held me close for a few moments and whispered for me to relax. He locked his eyes onto mine and began taking my clothes off until I was completely nude. My nipples were hard as rocks, not out of excitement, but fear. Tears welled up in my eyes, and I have no idea why.

Troy guided me to the bed and laid me down carefully. At first, he just stood there looking at me, but I could also see that he was pleased with this moment. He got into the bed and lay beside me, still staring. Kissing me gently and then with one hand, he began to caress me between my legs with his fingers and, at the same time, using his thumb to stroke my clitoris. His kiss was deep wet and thrusting inside my mouth. Pleasure set in as I began to forget what we were about to do, and shortly after that, Troy laid on top of me, holding both my hands gently above my head, and with his other hand, he maneuvered his member until it was able to penetrate inside of me. The pain was excruciating, and as a method to handle it, I began to suck on Troy's neck so hard and moaned softly," it hurts." He was still moving, although very gently; I just wanted it to be over. Tears rolled down my cheek, and I had to grab hold of this situation.

I kept telling myself, you are a woman, you can handle this, and he loves you. Troy never once stopped kissing me through the whole act as if to keep my mind occupied; it worked after a while. Yet and still, I was relieved when it was over. He came and was holding me so tight; I thought my body would break.

Kissing my nose, Troy looked into my eyes and said, "I love you, Zelda' I returned the words with tears in my eyes. The next thing I knew, I was waking up to a warm wet sensation between my legs. Troy was nursing me back to normalcy with the use of a warm towel to help ease the physical pain I had endured. I did it! I had given him the grand treasure, now all I needed was the great proposal.

However, it never came.

Like most of my days, I was going back and forth in the shopping district on Fordham Road, to window-shopping, of course. Troy believed shopping was the white's man way of making a black family broke. In two short years, Troy turned from a fun boyfriend to a pro-black activist, never wanting to partake in anything if he felt the white man was behind it. Well, I was a few months away from turning seventeen, and I was needy with no knowledge of how to get a job, acquire skills or support myself. For a moment, I couldn't help but entertain the thought of running out into traffic. Just end it. After all, what am I living for? My mother is who knows where, my boyfriend isn't trying to make me a wife, and to top it off, I have absolutely nothing except a few articles of clothing that barely fit. The emptiness was screaming loud, and just as I found myself at the corner, the light turned green. I contemplated deeply. However, no sooner, before I had finished my thoughts of loneliness' I saw her! My mother, across the street. Running as if traffic had no rules, I was lucky.

God did not let me get hit. "Mommy! "Mom, I yelled" She turned around and extended her arms to me as if to say I'm sorry.

She never once mentioned why she did what she did. As a matter of fact, she acted as if nothing had ever happened. (I realized later that guilt did and still does consume her). No words were necessary. That embrace healed so many wounds at that moment. "

You ready to come home?" was all she said. It was all she needed to say. As far as I was concerned, I had granted her forgiveness.

Life was going to be fantastic! My mother did love me! She wants me to come home! I put away all my grown-up mindsets and was eager to be a child. After all, the only reason. I grew so fast was for survival.

I grabbed a few things from the house and left Troy a "Dear John" letter thanking him for being my boyfriend and explaining that I wasn't ready for a relationship, and most importantly, I wanted to be with my mom. Then I headed to my mother's apartment, which ironically was only fifteen minutes away from Troy's. All this time, she was close by, and yet, I never knew it.

This beautiful mother and daughter bond will heal my wounds. I was still in high school, my grades went back up, and I found a bit of peace again. My mother and I never spent time together, and even though it was a one-bedroom apartment that she shared with an older woman whose daughter would shoot up dope in the hallway, and even though my mother had a female lover and we all three shared a full-size bed with me at the foot of it, I was back at home, and having mom being in the same household was sufficient for me to find a piece of happiness. I knew from that moment that life would be beautiful, and I would have a chance of normalcy.

Life was sweet for a whole three months. My grades were better than average now, and I felt significant. One Saturday morning, I decided to visit my friend from the old neighborhood to have something to do. Walking up the hill, I could see him from a mile away.

His name was Darren Witherspoon; he was my friend Brenda's brother. Darren was extraordinarily handsome and closer to my age. He was never a big talker, though. Perhaps his slight stutter made him stay on the quiet side.

"Hey Darren, how are you? Is your sister upstairs?" "I guess so," he replied. "Go up and see" "Can you go up first and put bullet away I stated with concern on my face. Bullet was their germen shepherd, and he was not the friendliest pet either. I never really liked big dogs; they seemed very threatening. "Ok, you big chicken," said Darren, "You scared of my dog?" "Yeah, I'm that" We both laughed as we began to walk up to five stories to Darren's apartment. I couldn't help but notice how nice he smelled. I waited in the hallway until he put his dog away then entered. It was fun feeling like a teenager again. I'm back with my mom; yeah, I was happy.

Darren and I had the kind of fun teenagers are supposed to have. We went to the park, the movies, window shopping, and holding hands. We laughed at each other's jokes; we shared soda pop from the same straw. No pressure, no wifely behavior. I could be normal. I found him intriguing because he looked so mature when he was silent, which turned me on.

Something about him gave me that I wish I were married to you feeling. He had a look of authority and was very mature. He never spoke any harsh words, and although he had a stutter, I understood every word he said. Darren Witherspoon and I dated for a whole three months, and it was blissful. His mom

37

allowed me to stay overnight because I was also friends with his sister, but she was not why I wanted to stay overnight. Darren Witherspoon was. That evening, everyone went to sleep except Darren and me. I asked if he would mind if I sat on his bed to watch television since I was not sleepy. He had no problem with that. In my mind, I was no longer with Troy; he did not ask to marry me even after a year of losing my virginity. I felt as if we were playing house, and I was not happy with that.

I was still seeking stability and love. Darren and I were watching television as if we were really interested in what Ralph Crandon was saying to   Alice on the Honeymooners. I do not know what made me lay in his bed that night, especially knowing his parents were there.

Darren did not seem to be bothered by my forwardness. In fact, he seemed to welcome it. Our night of intimacy was exciting, probably because we were sneaking it. The only thing that separated us from his parents was a sheet that divided the living room in which Darren slept and the parents' bedroom. I was sure that he would love me and one day marry me. I did not have to live with him; I could still be at home, finish school and have a boyfriend. I would have the perfect teenage life. I thought about college a lot, and I was going to be a psychologist. Being back home meant the opportunity for a normal life. I went to sleep feeling very content.

      In the morning, we moved from his bed to the couch to appear as if nothing had happened. We talked, and he knew about Troy, "So what are you going to do about this Troy dude?" "I'm not trying to share you with some guy" "I'm not really with him," I replied. "Yeah, but you still got stuff there." His eyebrows raised. "So, I will leave him a letter, and I don't think he's wondering about me at all."

      "So, you have me all to yourself" I was so gung-ho about having my mother in my life that closure never came to my mind. Troy never made me feel like he was all into me anyway; it felt more like pity, whereas Darren's emotion was more genuine. That morning Darren walked me halfway home. 'Darren, you don't have to walk me all the way home. I will be fine. "'What do you mean? I'm a gentleman; I'm not going to let you walk alone." You up to something you shouldn't be?" Darren said with a half-smirk and a raised eyebrow. "No," I laughed. "I'm just not comfortable with my house; it's a bit embarrassing." "Ok, if you feel that strongly about it, how about I just watch you walk till I can't see you anymore?"

      'Thanks,' I appreciate your understanding," and with that, I kissed him and told him I would see him tomorrow. Although I was excited to be with my mother, I did not want him to know she was gay and how we were living. Nor did I want to be if him in case I ran into Troy. I was not being a slut; if I was, it was not my intention. I was seeking to love; I was seeking to be loved and to matter.

He adhered to my reply and kissed me goodbye. "Until tomorrow. Then like every other significant moment in my life, it got shattered—just four months of being home and after a perfect night with Darren Witherspoon. Funny how God gives you a moment of bliss and yet, in an instant, takes it away as if to provide himself with aha moment.

By the time I reached the third level of our apartment, I had stood there, mouth wide open. There were padlocks on the door! I do not recall how I was feeling anything at that moment; a neighbor came up the stairs seconds later who was on her way into her apartment gave me that ole,

"Poor thing," look on her face as she said, "They put yawl out, and your momma said she was leaving the state; I thought you went with her. She left last night" I'm so sorry. With that, she put her head down and went into her apartment without so much as asking, is there a thing I can do to help you.

What! Are you fucking kidding me! Did I just get abandoned again! Not fury, not rage, nor anger set in. Whatever it was it had no name that I could think of at that moment. The only thing I was sure of was I could never continue my relationship with Darren Witherspoon. How could I tell him that I am officially homeless! I waited a few hours and headed back to his block. I watched him walk with his friends toward the opposite corner, and then, making sure he turned the corner to save myself the embarrassment, I ran upstairs and knocked on his door. His sister Brenda answered. "Who is it"? " It's Zelda," I replied. Brenda yelled through the door. "Let me put my dog bullet up," she said, laughing. She opened the door, and the tears fell down my face. "My mom left me" "What do you mean she left you" "What happened?" "I got home, and there were locks on the door, and her neighbor said she left the state" "Ah dam, I'm sorry," "You want to stay here?"

Brenda's mother was in the bathroom; when she came out, Brenda began to plea my case. "Ma, Zelda's mom left her. Can she stay with us?"
"Come here" Brenda's mother, Mrs. Witherspoon, motioned Brenda to the back in Brenda's room.

"She said no" said Brenda because she doesn't want other women around my father. "I'm sorry."

"It's ok, let me go and see where I'm going to lay my head today." I left, and when Brenda closed the door behind me, I could hear her mom yelling at her. I began to cry and felt very unwanted. Again. I would not be embarrassed again, so I never went back to Darren's house. I never saw him again, at least not for the next twenty-six years.

I am glad I made a choice not to tell him where I lived to save myself the shame.

I would not fail myself as she failed me, I thought to myself as I began to walk up toward Fordham Road, with a secret wish of seeing my mother again. I would finish school even if I had to wear the same clothes every day. I headed toward my grandmother's home, where my sister Cynthia was still staying, and then changed my mind after remembering that she said no the last time I asked to live there. I was just not in the mood for any more rejection. Perhaps, because she was conceived through rape is why even to the day, the family welcomed Cynthia. As for me, I was always told to work it out. Not always by actions but by words of things like, "you better start getting ready to go before it gets too late.

It only took a week of my little secret being found out by my school classmates that I was a minor living on the streets.

I stayed behind my school because of its location. It was a block from the city zoo, and in the evenings, you could hear the animals communicating. Growls, purrs, and chirps. Somehow, I found peace there. I also discovered my dinner in the trash that the school would dump daily, so it never had a chance to rot. I was selective, yes, but hungry more. As fate would have it, a classmate informed a security guard that she suspected something wrong with me, as did many other students. The officer was an older African American woman who was always considered strange but fantastic. During lunchtime, she approached me and offered me her couch to live with her.

Amazing how women, particularly those of color, have the biggest hearts in the craziest situations.

For a moment, she almost had me up until she gave me a piece of paper with a quote that she instructed me to read throughout the day until it was time to leave for the day. I agreed, and as she walked away, I opened the paper to read what it said. "NUM YOUNG HO RENGI KEYO." I'm not sure what it meant, but I was raised in the church, and whatever it was, it did not say Jesus, so I wasn't going to utter it. Had I known then what I understand now about meditation, I would have saved myself so much grief and heartbreak. Today, I not only practice meditation, but I teach it. I have mastered working faith with action, connecting to the creator, and, most notably, how vital meditation is. It's more like your spirit, not your flesh connecting with God. "Where was I?" "Oh yes," to not face this security officer with a heart of gold, I cut my last period class and left out the back door of the school. Later that same day, I ran into my classmate Tennille at the Pizza shop a few blocks from school. Tennille informed me that she and the others only told security out of concern, not malice.

I began to cry and told her my story. Tennille invited me to come over to her home; she said she was sure her mom would let me live there. She was right. Life had a chance, after all. Ms. Brenda was a sweet woman with a boyfriend who also resided there, yet I knew it would be trouble just by the way he looked at me.

I was happy inside when she was evicted two months later so that he never got a chance to finish what he attempted during the middle of the night when he thought everyone was asleep. Tennille and I moved in with her biological father. At first, I thought he was a cool cat. He did hair. He did mine. He had a girlfriend, and the environment felt like home.

The only disadvantage there was the family dog Trio. A ridiculously substantial lion-like family pet that looked like he ate the missing people you had seen on milk cartons. They were very understanding and kept him in the laundry room, so Trio and I never met face to face.

I was wearing Tennille's clothing as I had ownership of absolutely nothing. Most of her things fit me a bit snug since my breast and the rest of me filled out quite fully for a seventeen-year-old. Tennille continued going to school, and as for me, I chose to find a job; however, no one would hire me because of my age and lack of experience.

Therefore, I spent most of my time helping Tennille's father, Greg, at the hair salon. It was fun. All I did was sit at the desk and look cute, then sweep when hair hit the floor. Once again, getting the attention I did not ask for it was not long before Greg decided he would see just how far he could go. He went far, too far. Just doing what I was told, I went to the stock room to pull out shampoos and assorted items that would be needed for tomorrow's appointments. The shop was empty, but I never felt threatened by Greg; he never gave me a reason until that day. Standing on the six-foot ladder, trying to reach the deep conditioner case, I felt something up against my legs. It was Greg; at first, I thought he was simply trying to make sure I did not fall, yet he was stroking my legs!

I froze, unsure of what my next move should be. I tried to move, in my head, I was moving, but my body was not following! My foot managed to take a step down to leave as the environment turned hostile. "Where are you going?' "c'mon, you're a smart girl; you know if I'm paying you, you got to pay me." My ears could not believe what it was hearing! "I don't want," and before I could finish my thought of, I do not want to, Greg's mouth was locked around mine, tongue down my throat so hard preventing me from yelling. His grip on my arms prevented me from the slap I attempted to give him, and I don't know how but he managed to pin my arms behind my back and turn me around with such force.

I heard his zipper and felt my dress being lifted. The first thrust was so painful that the next thing I knew, I woke up on the couch of the stock room, my body was sore, and my face felt like a heavyweight champion punched it. A stabbing feeling came from my vagina as if a knife had been plunged and planted in me. Then it came back to me—fear set in quick as I attempted to pull myself together. I heard laughter in the shop, and nervously I walked out of the stock room into the shop. There was Tennille, Greg's girlfriend   Brenda, and the devil himself. "You feel ok, sweetie?" asked Brenda, "Greg said you had cramps, and that's why you were napping." I could not find any words to utter; I was trying to reveal what happened, but just as I found one word, "hurt," Tennille replies, "yeah, cramps hurt, girl, you are bleeding"! "You got to keep pads with you all the time because you never know when aunt flow is going to sneak up on yah."

I felt Greg's eyes piercing me, hypnotizing my strength. However, with everything in me, all I could do at that moment was run.

Stolen Virtue

I don't know how far I ran, I stopped when I realized people were stopping, and I heard someone say, "what's wrong with her" I ended up in the park where few people solicit at night and climb into the play trolley tube. You know, the one kids used to play hide and seek in. I placed my hand down there in such pain, covering it to protect it. Crackling sounds got louder, and then I realized it was beginning to rain. I screamed so loud, and God blocked my cry by allowing thunder to sound at the same time. Pull yourself together, I told myself. The first thing is to clean up. Well, it is pouring; make use of the water. No one was in the park, and there were enough bushy areas for me to go and take these panties off and wash in the rain.

When I was a child, my mother used to tell me the rain was God's tears. At that moment, all I could wonder was what did God have to cry over at this moment. I was afraid to take off my dress but felt it best to let it wash the best way I could. Therefore, I let the rain help me clean out the stains and put them inside the trolley. As if to do me a favor, God saw fit to be dry by morning, keeping me safe throughout the night and allowing me to appear as if nothing ever happened. At least on the outside, inside was a whole different story.

That following day, thoughts of yesterday ran through my mind, and while my mind wanted to report it to the cops, I remember what Greg said, you tell anybody, anybody at all, and I will find you! Nothing else, not I will kill you, nothing. It was that nothing else that petrified me. Manipulation is easy to behold when done to anyone minor or adult who is afraid. My silence gave me a guarantee of safety.

The streets would be my home for the next three months. Stealing to eat, going to the girls and boys club complimentary breakfast and lunch, since it was now summer break, washing in the showers of the city pool. It was free. Lonely was my best friend.

You would think that I should have had enough sense to go back to Karen's home, perhaps she would've taken me in, but so much shame took over me I couldn't bring myself to face her. Here I am, this child, this wildflower living in the streets of the South Bronx. No direction, no mentors, no nurturing. I felt so insignificant.

Envy crept on me so often as I watched young girls come and go, dressed in the latest Gloria Vanderbilt jeans and Puma sneakers. They look so happy. Where is my happiness? I asked myself frequently. My next thought was interrupted by a growl in my stomach as I realized I had not gone to the store to swap a few things to eat today. I hated stealing, I was taught you go to hell for that, but hell, it wasn't my fault my family wouldn't take me in. God owes me a few free passes, and I intend to collect.

Checking outside of the play tube I called home; I peeked out to make sure no one could see me coming out. Although the park was crowded during the day in the evening, it's empty except for a few feet away at the basketball court. The men there usually keep to themselves, probably because they do not know I am in here. I had no sense of time at this point; either the sun was up, or it was not. Quietly I crept out of the play tube and checked myself to make sure I didn't look too bad. I was still wearing the navy-blue dress I wore when I left Greg's salon. It carried a light odor but nothing significant enough to call attention to myself since, during my new talent of shoplifting, I now had a duffle bag, deodorant, four pairs of panties, and baby wipes. Simply necessities. I had not mastered stealing clothes yet.

To me, it was not necessary; I did not want anyone watching me, let alone admiring me in any way, form, or fashion.

I walked two short blocks away to the grocery store. One thing about the South Bronx is there is always an open store. Freddie's Grocery was the biggest store in the neighborhood with the freshest foods. There were about eight or nine people in the store when I walked in. No one was paying me any mind except for a little boy about three years old. "Stop starring"!

I thought to myself as if he could hear my thoughts.

Kids are a dead giveaway when you're up to no good. He looked as if to say, could you tell my daddy I'm ready to go? I returned the look to say, stop starring; you're going to get me caught! I walked down a few isles and slipped a pack of bologna under my arm underneath my dress to hide the bulge and grab a long Italian roll. Perfect, the customers were so busy laughing, talking about today's numbers and who hit.

One man I could see out the corner of my eye about sixty years old, with no teeth, waving his finger, which looked like he had been working on cars all day, laughed aloud, "you owe me fifty dollars' man pay the hell up," "I told you 118 was going to hit today; I dreamt it all fucking week." The laughter of excitement surrounded the store, and nobody even noticed I was in the store.

For a moment, I was hoping to be caught and have the owner just give me the food I had hidden so well so that I would not have to steal—no such luck. As I headed for the door, I snatched up fruit punch quarter water, and as I headed out, the little man waved goodbye! Dam! Freaking kids, but no one was paying him any mind either. I made it back to my home, so to speak, safety. I sat on the edge of the play tube, enjoying dry bread and bologna, and allowed myself to drift into a moment of fantasy. Closing my eyes, I pretended that I was in a real home at a dinner table, like back at Karen's house. There were brothers and sisters, a mother and father, and even a puppy. Instead of eating bologna on dry bread, I enjoyed fried chicken with white rice, green beans, and cornbread. However, just like every good moment, I managed to have while

God wasn't looking; he managed to wake up and take it away again. It was dark, and I could hear what appeared to be footsteps; oh.

God, I'm scared, I'm sorry I was stealing, I was just hungry, please protect me, don't let it be a dog! I could hear my heart racing like morning traffic. I held my breath to prevent any type of sound from coming from my sanctuary.

"Hey," I opened my eyes, an older, exceptionally clean man standing in the dark invading my space. "What do you want"

I replied, trying to sound unafraid. Freddie works just as hard as I do in that store you just stole from; why you are young butt out here instead of home where you

belong"?

"My business is my business," my mouth uttered with authority. "I don't know what you're talking about." His eyebrows gave me that parental look that doesn't play that with me. "The crumbs all over you say otherwise, now you stop being a smart ass and tell me why you out here by yourself, or you can tell the cops, pick one."

"Where's your mama"? "I do not know what it is about you young girls that you think you got all the answers trying to grow up before your time, running away from stupid shit into a cold world that could give a dam." "Your mama probably worried sick"!

He sounded so fatherly; my defenses went down.

"C'mon, I am taking you home; we will talk to your mom together." "You are not as grown as you think you are, and these streets got the kind of snakes you have never seen, nor do you want to." My head fell low, and the words jumped out before I could stop them" I don't know where she is"! She just left me; I didn't matter to her," I cried. His eyes looked like he just saw

Jesus.

"She did what" you stop that lying girl! I lifted my head and looked this man dead in his eyes, and in it, he saw my truth. I was alone. 'Well, don't you have a family looking for you? Surely somebody out there worrying about you?" They said they were not getting in it, was all I could say. My eyes swelled up like Niagara Falls, and I could not stop them; I was so tired, cold, and sick of stealing to eat. "My name is Mr. Edwin; come on, you can stay in my daughter's room for the night, and we will figure out what to do with you in the morning. "I am fine!" I yelled, "Hey, don't raise your voice to me, young lady; being homeless isn't an excuse for being disrespectful to your elder girl." I could not determine if he were safe or not, I was old enough to know not to go with a stranger, but I was too young to see if it was game. A child with a woman's body was all that I was. Mr. Edwin held out his hand and said," It's ok; I'm harmless and too old to want a child."

"You will be fine." "The way I see it is you come with me, or I call the cops because I'm not going to get any rest knowing you are living out here by yourself." I did not know what would happen if the cops got involved, but I knew if they did, I would have to tell them something, and I heard Mr.. Greg's voice, speaking in my head," tell no one"!

I submitted, hoping that I could find some peace in his care. Come to find out; he lived in the building across the street from the park. We walked up two flights, and he opened the door.

Something in my spirit said no, but my flesh was ever so tired. I just needed a place to call home a warm bed and a good night's sleep. Nevertheless, I will stay on guard. The apartment was very well kept for a man his age. He seemed to be somewhere in his fifties. His house was clean and dust-free, no pets, and there were pictures of the family hung all over the place. Yeah, he is safe. "I will heat up some spaghetti; you want some"? "Yes, Edwin, thank you." "Mr. Edwin to you, and what might your name be?" "Annie Mae." "Ok, Zelda, please meet you," He extended his hand for me to shake it, and I did. 'Let me show you where you will be sleeping; you can use my daughters' room; she's with her mama this week.

"It was any teenager's dream bedroom.

White walls with pink and stripe trim on the bottom base and pink stars on the ceiling. A full-size bed covered by a pink blanket and Janet Jackson plastered throughout the walls.

His daughter was an obvious fan.

By the clothes in her draws and closet, it was easy to see he takes care of his daughter. Yeah, he is safe. I just hope I have a good relationship with his daughter. When I think about it today, it never dawned on me as to why there was no picture of his daughter in her own room. I was so flabbergasted over everything else I missed that. He was the kind, sweet man who came and frequently went for three days. "Until we figure out what we are doing with you, I think it's best you stay indoors and don't talk to anyone." Ok, I replied, I don't want anyone asking me questions anyway.

Edwin left every morning and came back and forth constantly, sometimes with a friend or two, but any time, I heard the key in the door, and I scurried off to my room and stayed quiet. My third night in my new home was rainy; this normally would not be a problem as I am no chicken, but I don't like the sound of thunder. The sounds of thunder tonight were so loud and so frequent it was the end of the world, and Jesus was on his way back.

According to the neon pink clock in my room, it was close to morning when sleepiness started to settle in thunder or not. During those loud crackling sounds, I could have sworn I heard a tribe of pitter-patter steps. I also thought I heard a click, but as I said, sleep was more important to me. That morning, it seemed as if there had been no storm at all. The sun was bright, and I knew. Edwin was gone by now. He is normally gone before the sunrises. So, I grabbed an outfit from the closet (Mr. Edwin had always said his daughter wouldn't mind if I borrowed her clothes just take care of them), and in my attempt to open the door,

I couldn't it's stuck, perhaps. I began shaking it gently; those pitter-patter sounds were just confirmed, the door would not open, and the more I tried, the closer the pitter-patter sounds got to my door. I tipped toed back with fear as I could hear sniffing under the door. There was a dog in the house? There were several dogs in the house! Where did they come from? Why is the door locked? I jumped on the bed with the highest level of fear known to man and held my mouth to avoid crying aloud. It seemed like

hours before Mr. Edwin had come home. I had not used the bathroom, and really needed to go. I heard the door open, and his voice said, "Stay" A few steps shortly thereafter, he was in front of my door; it sounded like a bar being removed, then a latch, the door opened.

"Good morning, Zelda," I could not say anything at that moment, yet as he walked into the room, I got off the bed with the intent to use the bathroom.

Frozen in my steps as my eyes caught on to something that was not right, there was a shotgun; he was holding it down the side of his arm as if I would not notice. In all this fear, I looked down because there was something trickling down my legs. I had peed on myself. His mouth uttered a snicker. You grew you can't even hold your bladder." Before I could respond, those pitter-patters made themselves known. Two pit bulls. Big, black, healthy, and evident they did not like me based on the low growls that continued until Mr. Edwin said, "sit."

To keep some of my sanity as I write this, I will simply tell you that while many people laugh at my huge fear of dogs, this very moment in my life was the reason why. To be raped at gunpoint with dogs breathing in your face while you are on your knees can leave a hell of an imprint. I spent two days of this torture. My self-esteem was as shattered as my body. Being told I was too pretty to be taken seriously. In my moment of desperation, I was looking out the window of my room, and it hit me.

You can see the park where I used to sleep; even worse, you can see the play tube I had been resting my head. Had he been watching me the whole time? This was a plan, that bastard! I must get out of here! My head was all over the place, and I could find no solution in sight. I quickly added this event to my memory in my not liking God too much at this point.

As I look back, every time something crazy happened to me, God always showed me away after the fact. I never understood that. There was a side window in my room as well, and it led to the basement where people took their trash.

There was enough trash to land on if I had jumped, so I would not die, I thought to myself. I wrapped the blanket on the bed and hit the window real hard, but somehow it still managed to make a little nick on the side of my wrist while I was clearing some of the stuck glass. I positioned myself, asked God to watch me, and closed my eyes, then I did it; I jumped! It wasn't as bad as I thought it would be, I jumped up as fast as I could and ran in the opposite direction.

As I began to run, I realized I had nowhere to run to. Where was I going? I should have never left Troy; I should have never trusted my mother. Humiliation was closing in, but fear of being in the street was closing in more. My only other option was to hope that Troy would forgive me would let me back at home. I ran to Troy's apartment and knocked on the door. The tears fell before he even opened it. As if he knew what I had been through. Troy let me back home, no questions. This time he lived upstairs on his own.

We were not really dating, just existing in the same house. Although he said he still loved me, he was just showing human compassion.

Before I go any further, let me say this. In life, we have choices. While back then, my shame was greater of not being a virgin and fear of what may happen to my mother if the authorities found out I was abandoned, that I didn't go back to Mother Karen's home. Not that rape was ok, nor my fault. I had a choice, and I didn't choose right. Thus, I put myself in a victims' position.

A Survivor's Remorse

I took my life into my own hands and simply came and went as I pleased. I tried to get myself back into high school, but the principal, Ms. Rye, said it had been too long of me being out and that I would never be able to catch up. At that moment was when I felt anger; her white face telling the little black girl she was incapable of succeeding or meeting minimum requirements was an insult? Nose stuck up in the air, she bid me farewell and walked back into her office. Other teachers gazed at me as if I were worthless—a poor little black girl with no value.

If ever I have felt humiliation, this moment was it. Therefore, my time was spent window-shopping once again. I told Troy they would not let me back in school and he sort of shrugged and oh well. Just be home, cook, and clean, and I will take care of you. For about ten seconds, that sounded like the best news I could ever receive, then common sense jumped in my mind, and I heard, "be a fool if you want to" "Ok, thank you, I said." In the back of my mind, I would find out what I could or should do for my current situation. Months went by, as playing wife had gotten boring, I began feeling incomplete. There was a void still building up inside, as I did not know how or with what to fill it with.

New Year's once again was here, and it was time to do something different with Troy although I was grateful, I am outgrowing him and felt as I was stuck, I was moving nowhere really fast with no purpose. Quickly! Therefore, while we were riding on the A train, heading to his grandmother's house to be with family, I decided I was going to visit the cousins I had in Queens instead. Sure, I have not seen them in forever, but they are there most likely, and right now, I needed a change. Certainly, I was seeking some sense of belonging. I realized as I write that everyone goes through something, and I was not alone. Perhaps, I should have said something looked for them months ago, maybe talked to them more, but shame embraced me hard. It was obvious Troy was pissed, but hey, either go with me or leave me alone. Still, a mind of my own cannot be changed by anyone unless I allow him or her. This was exceedingly rare.

I got off the train to head on my own to Lefrak City in Rego Park, and as luck would have it, my cousins were getting dressed to go to a house party! Just what I needed; I must let my hair down. I was lucky enough to wear the same size as my cousins, and they made me look stunning. My little secret would remain mine as I sought normalcy and excitement for the evening.

We arrived in Harlem and entered the party, and all eyes were on me. Oh yes, did I mention that I changed my clothes, from the blue slacks and red top to a black back-out spandex dress with open-toe shoes? A real head-turner.

Come to find out; it was also some guy's birthday; a challenge overcame me when one of my cousins informed me that this playa came with three women, so don't even attempt to get his attention.

One thing dangerous about me was that I loved a challenge. Even after all I had been through, there was a character developing within, and I can't say if she was a good one yet; I can say this, she is a survivor. All I did was walk past this tall, dark, and handsome man. He had to be at least six feet tall, but that did not mean much to me, considering I was a mere four feet eleven inches, so everyone was tall to me. I simply looked dead in his eyes and said happy birthday. "Who are you"?

He asked," I am tiny,"

(We all had play names that fit our character back in the day) Carol's cousin. "Come and dance with me he ordered." Ok, I thought to myself, he's aggressive. (Hint number one that I disregarded) A little sidestep, don't want to look like I am one of these hoochies, I thought to myself. Then it happened, the DJ put on reggae, and if any of you know anything about reggae, it's the music of seduction. It did not take a rocket scientist to notice the sway in my hips and my nipples protruding through my dress. Long story short, Travis came with three women, but left with me. Although looking back once again, this was a warning sign; I ignored it. So, into seeking to be loved and feel significant, I went with the first person that showed interest. Another dangerous move we ladies do in this thing called life. I never officially moved out of Troy's house; I just never went back. I was now old enough to babysit my little cousin, and her mom would pay me a few dollars. Now for a while, I have a safe roof over my head. It was a no-brainer and the beginning of a new life for me.

Travis called me two and three times a day just to say hello.

"Move in with me," he asked; light bulbs went all through my head, and I never playhouse, and no sooner than I thought it, I

ended up with the reply, "give me a few months to find a job."
The reaction of disappointment fell upon Travis's face. "A few
months"! He replied, "I want to come home to you every day,
girl; stop playing." A part of me was afraid because Travis, just
like Troy, was older. In fact, Troy was seven years older, and
Travis was eleven years older than I was. However, the thought
of stability and someone to love me was my greatest desire. Just
love me, which was all I ever wanted then and even now. Just
love me. Nervous, yet willing and hopeful for love, I moved in at
the end of the month, but not before stopping at Troy's house to
get my belongings. Troy stood at the door and just watched this
man, 6'2 tall, load my bags into his Cadillac, and he did not even
utter a comeback like, I love you, or I want you to stay, let's work
it out. What a waste of time; you are not even willing to question
why I'm leaving, what's the point of staying. That was January;
by Valentine's Day, the ole girl was wearing an engagement ring
and taking care of Travis's ten-year-old, that came to live with us.
The traits of wickedness were not easy for me to see. My whole
family loved Travis. He could do no wrong. We spent endless
nights of romance on the beach; he showered me with gifts that
said I love you, and I appreciate you. We barbecued almost every
week. Travis was the kind of man that if a child was hungry, he
would feed them. Travis was admired by the whole

neighborhood. He was a perfect caregiver, lover, and friend.

There was only one thing I picked up that really bothered me. On several occasions, I had overheard how abrasive he spoke to his mother. This made me uncomfortable, but I wasn't sure how to approach him about it. It was small things like if she fell, and he had to go and pick her up, he would scream and curse about her clumsiness. I think he was just frustrated and hurting about the fact that she was becoming sick. Perhaps he just didn't know what to do. While in my mind, I should have taken this as a warning, I took it and turned it into an excuse for him. It never dawned on me that this is the characteristic trait of an abuser. However, I was in love.

So, in my attempt to "fix" the problem (I was always trying to fix someone else's issues, never seeing my own.) I would take care of her. I would get to her before he would have to. I would bathe her, and as she became older and sicker, I would change her soiled garments. It broke my heart, and I wasn't sure what I was supposed to do; I had only been Nineteen for a few months. I am still learning how to be a stepmother. Clueless, yet I cared about Travis so much. I closed my eyes to the warning signs. It did not click in my head that any man that curses out his own mother is not a good helpmeet for any woman. One minute he was mister smooth; the next minute, he would turn into the coldest thing on ice. Four months into the relationship, I found out I was pregnant. I was shocked because I was told I would never be able to have children after the rapes. However, it would be after my son was born that I would see the devil rear his head in the man who used to sing to me, hold me laugh with me, and make me feel I was his all. He was drunk, which was not new; I had noticed that Travis drank more than I cared for and used a few things for which I did not care. During one of those drunken nights, Travis had his best friend over for drinks. I sat on the floor in front of the television, holding my new and precious miracle son. Minding my own business, ignoring all the foolishness of male chatter that was behind me. Why don't they go into the living room? I thought to myself. However, since Travis and Bernie were best friends and the only T.V. in the house was in the bedroom. Travis always allowed him in our marital room to have male chatter and watch sports.

Careful not to think aloud since Travis was drunk. When he got that way, I made it my business to keep my distance. A dirty sock from out of nowhere came over my shoulder

onto my son's face.

I honestly thought he threw it at me and simply missed, but no, he was aiming at my baby! What the hell? He threw it again, and this time, when I moved it off my baby's face, where it landed. Before I could put the sock on the floor, I felt a blow come straight to my face!

Travis was 6' 2 to my 4'9, and nothing was small on him, so needless to say, that slap was painful. 'Did I fucking tell you to move it?" he yelled! I was shocked and scared all at the same time. Did this man just hit me? He threw the sock again as I was standing up, so it missed my son. Travis lunged toward me, and went to grab my son, Bernie, who was shocked as well, got between us to prevent that from happening.

I took my son and ran to another room for both our protection. I had no idea what my next move would be, but I knew for our safety, I would have to leave. Lack of knowledge and a place to live prevented me from moving fast enough, and so I would be with him a few more years and endured being beaten and humiliated in front of neighbors and other women he brought in my presence. I don't know what or why the change in him took place. At first, we were a beautiful family, next thing I was preparing myself to welcome a beast home who drank excessively and got joy telling his friends my flaws. I cooked, we barbecued, and in between, I watched his mother being verbally abused by him, and while I tried my best with little knowledge or experience as a caretaker, bathed her, changed her adult pampers, and cleaned her mattress when she had accidents. She eventually went to glory while I was stuck with Satan's son.

Like many women foolish enough to try to create a pleasant moment despite our circumstances, I would try to be a better wife hoping I could change him. What did I know at 20 years to his 31 years of wisdom? Like most, I believed I could change him, make him love me as he used to. That mindset didn't last long.

I was really getting tired of trying to build a family with a man who flirted with other women in my face as I was his sister instead of his fiancé.

"You ready to tie the knot with me?" "I couldn't believe my ears. This came out of nowhere. 'Ah, sure, when you want to do it?"

Let's go to the courthouse tomorrow."

Foolishly, my mind told me, he was ready to be good, and I went along with it. I told myself, since the women he cheated on me were such a low grade, perhaps he was ready for the quality he had that laid beside him.

I was the winner. Perhaps, the good Lord was going to bless me after all with happiness.

Short-lived blissful moment, as I discovered just about every male guest was getting a blow job in my bathroom from the neighborhood crack head, at my home reception that I had prepared all by myself while he was out drinking the night before, including my new husband. 'What the hell!" 'Travis, What the hell is your problem?" "Babe, it wasn't me; I was telling her to leave" 'C'mon now, why the hell would I do that in my own house, especially with you here?" "It's our wedding reception, really, baby; I love you more than that. Naturally, everyone was saying the same thing, "no, it wasn't Travis, it was the other guys," etc. So, I shook it off my shoulder, but I put it in my memory bank, just in case. A week had passed, and there was a gentle breeze in the summer air that night that I decided to create a romantic atmosphere for my darling first husband and enjoy my new marriage tonight since I never got to wear it on my reception eve since Travis was so drunk that night. I had just purchased a black silk strapless teddy, which I got on sale at Victoria Secrets, with matching thongs that enhanced the curves of my ass cheeks, I was quite proud of. (I was wondering if wearing a thong might send the wrong message, Travis has been trying to get up in my ass for a while now, but it is just not my thing). Hubby is on his way home from work, so I have about 45 minutes to get everything set up for the perfect night of sweet sweaty passionate sex.

For the record, I have also learned that if no one is sweating, there is not much work being done. For the record, it is a very erotic image to see a body glossy, especially in a woman's neck area. In any event, I decided that this evening, I would do things sexually that I am against; it's not humiliating or anything; I just do not prefer swallowing shit that doesn't belong in my stomach. It has always been my practice to masturbate before I have sex. I think it was to make myself feel in control so that I was not feeling from them but from myself. This was, I think, the imprint of rape from the past. (Not that Travis was bad or anything, although he could use a book or two) As a young woman, I am in tune with my body; the only other woman I can think of that understands my sexuality is Janet Jackson. It was about passion. When I listen to her, I can feel myself; my hands do not have to think they know just where to touch. The fragrance of choice; white roses, I am turned on by the fragrance, and as I look at myself in our body-length mirror, my body turns me on. My perfect round breast and erect nipples, the curves on my waist, and even the little scar from my cesarean from the birth of my son turned me on as I applauded myself for being able to conceive, although the doctors said I could not.

My lips, pink and perfect, I press my body onto the mirror with suds and hot water being my caresser; I feel my body beginning to throb. Watching my body, by using my mind, I am coming close. Yet, with all that you have just read, it was never about feeling good physically; it's always been about me being in love with me, truly, because no one else would. It was my tool for inner peace. No man that has ever touched me made me feel this way, and I realize it was because they could never love me as I love me. Travis came home from work still in his uniform, and he had a strange look on his face, but I disregarded it, for this will be a night of passion; hell, I may even let him have my ass tonight. Walking slowly toward him, I unbutton his shirt and begin kissing his chest, using my hands to stroke his manhood to see if he is ready. He is not. I am going to have to give him a hand. Undoing his pants, I kneel slower than a turtle (it is all about presentation); we've been married for many years now, and I try to stay fresh in my ideas, nothing more dangerous than a boring sex life.

As I land on my knees, I begin unzipping (in the back of my mind, I can't understand why he isn't erect yet, dam what's the problem?). No sooner than the thought came into my mind, a loud piercing rang in my ears, and in less than a second, I was laid out on the floor!

The last time this happened, Travis said it would never happen again. This time my common sense made me get up and fight back, knowing I could not win, but my ego was bruised, as was my face. My beautiful face. That's it; I am done.!

It should have been apparent to me that if a man can use profanity at his own mother because of her infirmities, he would be of little use to a woman, let alone a wife. But I was young and naïve and thought I was in love. The truth was actually I was in love with the possibility of having someone love me. The whole scene of the family was a fervent desire within my heart, and I thought I could change him and make him a part of my life.

Reality sets in hard when your body is in pain and, more so, when your ego is hurt, and when your self-esteem is crushed, you will find a way to get out.

My family did not want to get involved and even stayed friends with him to this day! To them, he's such a wonderful man and a great father. Good father, yes, wonderful man, hmm, I don't think any man that yells at his mama with profanity and beats his wife and has sex with crack heads and low lives in our bed is a wonderful anything.

I have taken enough, but how can I get out? Where can I go? I have never had a job in my life. I have always been the caretaker to his mother and our children.

But my heartache would not stop there. No, there was much more to happen to hurt me before I would find the sunshine.

'Tony, you seen my husband?'

(Tony was Travis's buddy from up the street. I had just come back from the supermarket. For the last five months, it's been very quiet as far as the domestic abuse goes. However, that didn't stop other types of pain from occurring. The kind that's hard to re-build your self-esteem from)

"Yeah, he up at Rogers crib; you want me to get him?" "Nah,

I'll get him," I replied. "I had that feeling that the whole neighborhood was watching me head up the stairs to Roger's house. Tony ran past me like a bolt of lightning.

"Yo Travis, your wife here, man"! By the time I reached the top of the steps, I could see inside once Tony had gone in. The scent of filthy sex of something unclean was in the air, and my heart had already started pounding against my chest. Butterflies had already begun spiraling in my belly, and I didn't know if I was about to be pissed, angry, or hurt.

But I knew this wasn't going to be good.)

No sooner than I stepped my foot in the house, I saw her run like hell into the bathroom; Roger closed the door and stood in front of it as if to protect her. His pants were undone, Travis's penis sticking out, and cum still on it from whatever nasty bitch was just on it. It was obvious he was high, and there was some sick shit going down in this little trio. "Bitch, you're going to have to come out that bathroom sooner or later, and trust me, I will see you"! "Yo you, babe, why you are screaming, said Travis, "ain't nothing going on in here" "Dude please, you can't even speak straight" "you think I'm stupid, what! I'm not fucking you enough you got to come up the street."

Move out of my way, Roger!" I screamed, "Bitch, I will kick your ass on principle alone."

I was too angry to be hurt. That would come later.

Pulling on the doorknob handle, Roger would not budge.

'C'mon, baby girl, she isn't even worth all this," said Roger.

"Neither one of you are, but that's not the dam point," I yelled. Turning around, my eyes locked in on Travis, who was so high that he was clueless about what was happening. "You nasty son of a bitch" Raising his hands to hold me, I pulled back. His eyes rolled back, and he began to smile. He was not present in the situation, so as his wife, I felt it my responsibility to wake him the fuck up with a hard-core slap across the face.

By the time I reached the street, it was evident that the whole block knew exactly what was going on and was waiting to see the outcome. "Any more of you low bitches, want to go and fuck my husband, go right ahead"! I yelled. It took all my energy not to cry, especially with everyone watching me. I would not give them satisfaction. The only thing I could do at this point was tolerate the humility and find a job as soon as possible. I didn't have time to be hurt or angry, I had a son who relied on me, and so my feelings would stay inside and bleed till further notice.

THE DO-OVER

The first thing I did knew I had to do was create a false resume and have the few loyal friends be prepared to answer the phone as my former bosses. It worked! I got a job! Oh, it is on now, the pay was small yet big enough to help me find my self-esteem that had been ripped from me without my consent. I became a cook in the local jail. Fear set in at first being around so many convicts, but we were very protected by the officers.

My sister worked there as an officer, so fear came and went fast. She showed me the ropes and introduced me to some of the other officers, instructing them to watch my back. One officer caught my eye, Steve Walkers. Officer

Walkers was the most arrogant man I had ever met, although he had the right to be, because when I say DAMN!

This man was fine as hell!

Perfect posture and broad shoulders, it was the age of Jerri curls, and he wore it well. As hungry as I was since Travis, and I were not having sex anymore I mentally drooled at the thought of lying down with Steve. I would sit and wonder, was he someone who fucked or was he a love maker? No sooner than I thought about it, Steve turned and looked at me as if he heard me. Yeah, I think he does both. I laughed to myself. When he got on my line for me to serve him, I could not help but flirt.

'What would you like" I would ask, and I was not talking about the menu, and he knew it. He would always laugh and give me that "yeah ok" look. I was serious. I wanted to him. Sometimes his post was in the kitchen so when I took lunch, I could not help but mentally make love to him.

I would see him in the employee gym, so I know his

packing. Never stare at a person while they were eating, that's rude. However, I can surely position myself so that if my eyes were open, they would be looking at him. Nevertheless, they were closed so it did not count. His thick black hands cupping my breast, which of course are surely developed at this point. Nipples erect and ready for his mouth that teases me with words that have hidden meaning. My mind got really carried away today, I see his naked brown body and mine, both complexions glisten under the moonlight, eyes connected speaking without words of I want you. His lips coming closely to my partially opened mouth; breathing heavily and I was eager

to taste his tongue. The cool flavor of mint that he is

always sucking, yet this time he would be sucking me instead of the mints. In my lunchtime fantasy, Steve knew how to penetrate with a gentleness for which I have always longed. The kind that says this is not fucking, I am making love to you.

The alarm went off right in the middle of my fantasy and reality set back in that I was in a jail not a bedroom. It's crazy that all the while that the kitchen staff including myself took our prospective positions to the corner of the kitchen as we should when an alarm goes off, I could still see Officer Walker suiting up. It turned me on just watching him move with authority. Now that is a bad boy. A man who manages business with authority not that shit they roll with today.

No, Steve was turning me on, and we were connecting several times a day. In my mind anyway.

A simple night out with co-workers is what got me and Steve to be closer friends. "Hey, you want to give me your number maybe we can hang out sometime?" Asked Steve. "I'm married" I replied. "What! He got you out here by yourself looking like that. "'What the hell wrong with him?" He chuckled. "Long story" I said, trying to keep my face straight. "Well, tell you what; if you ever want someone to talk to, call me" We can be friends." Friends! I thought to myself, man, you don't know what I'm

thinking to myself" "Ok," I said, I'd like that. For months, Steve and I were platonic friends; he gave me a brighter perspective on men.

That not all men where vicious dogs that need to be put

down. Steve and I continued to be platonic friends, and perhaps it was because he kept his distance other than a few sexual jokes, it made me want him more. We had the kind of relationship that I could spend the night, and nothing happened. He was becoming increasingly attractive to me because he was so caring. He became the man I could go to and vent when Travis and I had problems. I was still with Travis, but only until I could save up enough money to move out. Divorce was already being planned that I may have a better life. In the back of my mind, I was hoping I would have a life with Steve. A few months had gone by and somewhere between my brother's wedding and Memorial Day, the girls and I got very drunk and yes, I screwed my husband. I cannot say I remember the details; I rather forget. For that moment of hell, I was however, rewarded with a beautiful baby girl. There was a moment that we got along and act like married people. Happily, married people at that. Yet in the back of my mind, it was already set-in stone that I was leaving him, and I would continue being close friends with Steve. I would wait until every duck was lined up. After all, I still had an eight-year-old son to take care of. Steve had a girlfriend, and we would discuss our relationship issues with each other almost daily if not weekly. He was also

my sister's friend so whenever we had a family function

Steve was there. He became Uncle Steve to the little ones and big bro to everyone else. How could I not love him? How could I even get him out of my head when he was everywhere?

Eventually, those nights of sleeping over without sex turned into nights of erotic passion.

Other nights, he would leave me at his house by myself because he had a date. However, not before running me a bath, feeding me, and kissing me goodbye. "I will be back in a few hours. You straight?" He would always ask. "I'm good" I replied. "Make sure you wrap it up," I said laughing." You funny," said Steve" Then out the door, he went, either on a date or to hang with the fellas. During my pregnancy with my unborn daughter, I got extremely sick. The first person I called was my buddy

Steve. "Hey Steve, what are you doing?" "Just laying here chilling, why?" what's up?" Nothing, I have the flu, in the worst way, and you can't take medication while pregnant so I'm trying to tough it out. "Where's the ole dude at? He ain't taking care of you?" 'Yeah right, he outside talking to the chicken heads up the block as always. 'Call a cab and bring your ass here, I got something for you." Nah, I'm good, but thanks" "Don't make me bust your shit, get your ass over here" (that was Steve's favorite line) 'ok, I'm coming" My fever was high, and my energy was low therefore I could not get myself to look cute. I threw on a sweat-suit, called a cab, and stood outside waiting for out.

"Later" yelled Travis, watching me from up the street. Not even concerned about where I was going. I could have been on my way to the hospital, he could care less. Naturally, there were ate least three bitches sitting with him. At this point, it didn't bother me, it was not about love anymore with

Travis, it was about survival and security for my children. Being pregnant did not bother Steve at least not that he ever mentioned. We never had sex during my pregnancy, and perhaps because of that is when I began developing feelings for him. When I got to his house, Steve treated me like not only his best friend but also a Queen. He sponged me done occasionally to get the fever down. Gave me Tylenol and made me breakfast in bed. I could not eat of course, but when a man gives you his bed to lie in, sits on the floor cutting up potatoes for you, and makes the full breakfast,

fruit, and all, it kind of opens your eyes to what you have before you.

He was not arrogant at all. He was confident, he was sincere, and he was real, and he was confident. Yet and still with all that time we spend, He still would not make me his. Call me a fool, but even knowing I still hoped. He had card blanch to my heart and though many times I would tell myself to stay away from him, I could not, I would not. I was in love with a man while married to another and yet the man I loved deserved me more. Mind-body, soul, and I wanted to be there to give him just that.

Steve was building up in my heart and this was a dangerous friendship. We understood that we were not a couple, but more like best friends with benefits. This is just what we are. Yet as painful as it was, I wouldn't change a thing. I would need an intervention quick otherwise; I would live a life of loving without having. What speed up the process of moving out, was the reminder of how much of a dog Travis was. His mother died, and while I was carrying my unborn child of nine months, I stepped outside to see if this man had any mourning going on that he may need my shoulder to cry on. There he was, kissing another woman right in front of our house. Travis turned and looked at me with a smirk, grab her waist and they walked up the road toward the funeral home. Un-freaking-believable! But then again not really. Travis was many things and cold and heartless was one of them. It only took thirty days after the death of my mother-in-law to plant a seed of motivation to move out, have better, and be better. I managed with the help of my sister to get an apartment in her name. A beautiful studio, ironically in Rego Park,

Queens of all places, the same complex I met Travis in. Ironic I'd say. It would appear life was trying to tell me something but at that moment, I had no clue as to what that message was.

I still had my job as a cook at the county jail in Brooklyn, and Steve and I were still very much connected at every opportunity. I kept myself extremely busy to keep him out of my mind. Most people would consider our relationship a booty call, however, the only difference here was I had developed feelings for him. The only thing we never did together was share holidays like Christmas and Thanksgiving.

However, I heard from him on Valentine's Day, always got a gift and when we were together you would swear the way he treated me we were dating. However, we were not and not because I did not want to. He would often change the subject when it came up. Therefore, I allowed myself to be a part of this love circus in an attempt to rid me of my loneliness and held on to faith as if it would make things change. At this moment, I have come to realize that even faith cannot deliver to you that which is not meant for you.

However, faith will remove you from where you should not be to where you ought to be. I quit my job as a cook after a brief time when I was unable to change to the day shift. Driving in to work at 2 a.m. just was not safe and it was getting harder to find a sitter once my sitter had to quit to return to school. I was, however, able to find a job shortly thereafter. I would use my time wisely in hopes of getting Steve out of my heart.

I soon took a job at one of the most popular electronic stores in Brooklyn, so we were always, busy and sales were great. My commission check along with my paycheck was sufficient for me to have a great babysitter, a furnished studio and some really fly suits and dresses. If you looked at me, you would swear I had a perfect life, my dirty little secrets of abuse, abandonment, and rape was buried deep within, although, at night, the memory of my reality was evident the moment the kids went to sleep. I could not help but cry. Constantly. I was still in a lot of pain; I just was not during it. I had my own. There was no one here to hurt me. My children now needed me and there was no room to be weak. Eventually, I got promoted from sales to Cash   Office Manager.

I made a promise to myself that they would never see hunger or worry about where they were going to sleep at night. By the grace of God, I would build a home for them despite my past.

My hours were long yet beneficial so I would not complain. Paul was one of the older security officers who took his job profoundly serious. Very handsome and probably around fortyish, He always wore a suit and smelled like expensive cologne. A few times, I could feel him staring at me from the corner of my eye, but I assumed he was just doing his job. I really did not take it any further than that. Hell, I had enough going on and I was not looking for anybody.

My new position as Cash Office Manager began tonight so there is no way I can leave yet. I made a call to Mary my babysitter who was so excited for me and told me to take the night. "Take the night" what do you mean? "Girl, I have watched you hustle since you moved in this building, you keep the kids clean and fed and you have them outside every day.

You're a great mother." "I do not want to get in your business, but with all I see you do, you could use a break.

There is no school it is Friday, go celebrate or hell go home and get some rest. You can leave them here and pick them up tomorrow, just make sure you get them by 11 am because have errands ok." 'Oh, Mary thank you, but you do not have to do that." "Stop it girl, I got you. I'm hanging up now, go live a little or sleep a lot, it's up to you." Wow, that was a beautiful thing for Mary to do. When I got off the phone, I realized all the staff had gone except for Bernard, the head of the electronics department. He was always making sure things were prepared for his area for the next day. Bernard was a genius. He was moving around his area while talking with Paul. Whatever they were talking about was funny and private for when I walked closer, they stopped talking. Both looking at me with Kool-aide smiles.   "Hey new boss lady" stated

Bernard, then Paul bust out laughing. "I'm sorry I'm sorry, I'll be nice." "Bernie, you should have been there no matter what she said, Zelda's words were like, "look you lazy chicken head, I got your job now get to stepping!" (Referring to the old Cash Office Manager that got fired tonight, I was the new head) (Both laughing) "Hey now, be nice," I stated. "Anyway, Bernard, don't you take the F train right/ well could you do me a favor and wait for me so I'm not riding by myself." However, the only thing is when you are done, you will have to clock out is that ok?"

"I will only be about 10 minutes," I turned to Paul, and the deposit is set already for the bank so we will be out of here quick.

Bernard opened his mouth to respond but Paul jumped in," the only problem with that is that I'm taking Paul home tonight after we make the deposit." "Oh ok," before I can get any other words out, Paul continues, "it's Friday, I can drop you off too, it's no problem. Where you live?" I smiled and said I live in Queens, but that is ok, I am not a party buster, I will be fine. Plus, I don't want any trouble with your girl." Why did I say that!

The laughter in the room was addictive and loud." My girl! In what fairy tale?" Bernard almost choked, he laughed so hard. "Ok then, let us all play nice. Let me get to work, it's way too much drama." Smiling at the two, I headed upstairs to finish and just as I said I was 10 minutes and done. As we pulled the gate down, we all headed to the bank to make the deposit.

Funny I never paid Paul any mind until tonight. To see him walking tall with authority, hand on his gun, walking behind me with Bernard. I never paid any real attention, but I could smell his cologne, he wore

Obsession. I felt so protected. Hmm, no, I'm not messing with that, too much going now in my life I thought to myself. Paul and Bernard talking as if I were not there, making it easy to quickly remember my position there as an employee not a friend. After the deposit we headed toward to the store, the train station was at the corner, and the guys were still talking. "Night fellas," I said as I turned to wave while they were walking behind me.

"Oh, now c'mon, I'm not going to let you take the train it's 11:30 at night! I don't bite," affirmed Paul, "at least not hard," laughed Bernard. "Stop before you scare the woman." "Zelda look, let's take Bernie home, and then I will take you home, you'll be in good hands." I have nothing else to do I thought to myself. "Ok" I agreed.

We proceeded an extra block down to Paul's car. "Nice!" I spoke. A great dresser, good taste in cologne and a badass car.

"Paul, can I be nosey?" Opening the door for me, replying, "Go ahead, shoot" "You work part-time at the store and yet," but before I could ask, there goes Bernie, how you got this nice stuff man. We could not all help but to laugh aloud.

I work in law enforcement as well Zelda. 'Oh, I was just wondering" I said as I smiled at him getting into the car.

To see him walking tall with authority, hand on his gun, walking behind me with Bernard. I never paid any real attention, but I could smell his cologne, he wore Obsession.

I felt so protected. Hmm, nope, I am not messing with that, too much going now in my life I thought to myself.) Zelda look, let us take Bernie home, and then I will take you home, you'll be safe." I have nothing else to do I thought to myself. "Ok" I agreed. We proceeded an extra block down to Paul's car. "Nice!" I spoke. A great dresser, good taste in cologne, and a badass car. "Paul, can I be nosey?" Opening the door for me, replying, "Go ahead, shoot" "You work part-time at the store and yet," but before I could ask, there goes Bernie, how the hell you got this nice stuff man. We could not all help but to laugh aloud.

The first thing I knew I had to do was create a false resume and have the few loyal friends be prepared to answer the phone as my former bosses. It worked! I got a job! Oh, it is on now; the pay was small yet big enough to help me find the self-esteem that had been ripped from me without my consent. I became a cook in the local jail. Fear set in at first, being around so many convicts, but we were very protected by the officers around us.

My sister worked there as an officer, so fear came and went fast. She showed me the ropes and introduced me to some of the other officers, instructing them to watch my back. One officer caught my eye, Steve Walkers. Officer Walkers was the most arrogant man I had ever met, although he had the right to be because I say DAMN!

This man was fine as hell!

Perfect posture and broad shoulders, it was the age of Jerri curls, and he wore it well. As hungry as I was since Travis and I were not having sex anymore, I mentally drooled at the thought of lying down with Steve. I would sit and wonder, was he someone who fucked, or was he a love maker? No sooner than I thought about it, Steve turned and looked at me as if he had heard me. Yeah, he does both, I laughed to myself. When he got on my line to serve him, I could not help but flirt.

'What would you like" I would ask, and I was not talking about the menu, and he knew it. He would always laugh and give me that "yeah, ok" look. I was serious. I wanted him. Sometimes his post was in the kitchen, so I could not help but mentally make love to him when I took lunch.

I would see him in the employee gym, so I know his packing. Never stare at a person while they are eating; that's rude. However, I can surely position myself so that if my eyes were open, they would be looking at him. Nevertheless, they were closed, so it did not count. His thick black hands cupped my breast, which is indeed developed at this point. Nipples were erect and ready for his mouth that teased me with words that have hidden meaning. My mind got carried away today; I see his naked brown body and mine, both complexions glisten under the moonlight, eyes connected speaking without words of I want you. His lips came close to my partially opened mouth, breathing heavily, I was eager

to taste his tongue. The cool flavor of mint that he is constantly sucking, yet this time he would be sucking me instead of the mints. Steve knew how to penetrate with the gentleness I have always longed for in my lunchtime fantasy. The kind that says this is not fucking; I am making love to you.

The alarm went off right in the middle of my fantasy,

and reality set back in that I was in a jail, not a bedroom. It's crazy that all the while that the kitchen staff, including myself, took our prospective positions to the corner of the kitchen as we should when an alarm goes off, I could still see Officer Walker suiting up. It turned me on just watching him move with authority. Now that is a bad boy. A man who manages a business with authority, not that shit they roll with today.

No, Steve was turning me on, and we were connecting several times a day. In my mind anyway.

A simple night out with co-workers is what got me and Steve to be closer friends. "Hey, you want to give me your number. Maybe we can hang out sometime?"

Asked Steve. "I'm married," I replied. "What! He got you out here by yourself looking like that. "'What the hell wrong with him?" He chuckled. "Long story," I said, trying to keep my face straight. "Well, tell you what; if you ever want someone to talk to, call me" We can be friends." Friends! I thought to myself, man; you don't know what I'm

thinking to myself" "Ok," I said, I'd like that. Steve and I were platonic friends; he gave me a brighter perspective on men.

That not all men were vicious dogs that needed to be put down. Steve and I continued to be platonic friends, and perhaps it was because he kept his distance other than a few sexual jokes; it made me want him more. We had the kind of relationship that I could spend the night, and nothing happened. He was becoming increasingly attractive to me because he was so caring. He became the man I could go to and vent when Travis and I had problems. I was still with Travis, but only until I could save up enough money to move out. Divorce was already being planned that I may have a better life. I was hoping I would have a life with Steve in the back of my mind. A few months had gone by, and somewhere between my brother's wedding and Memorial Day, the girls and I got very drunk, and yes, I screwed my husband. I cannot say I remember the details; I rather forget. However, I was blessed with a beautiful baby girl for that moment of hell. There was a moment when we got along and acted like married people. Happily, married people at that. Yet, in the back of my mind, it was already set-in-stone that I was leaving him, and I would continue being close friends with Steve. I would wait until every duck was lined up. After all, I still had an eight-year-old son who relied on me. Steve had a girlfriend, and we would discuss our relationship issues almost daily, if not weekly. He was also

my sister's friend, so Steve was there whenever we had a family function. He became Uncle Steve to the little ones and big brother to everyone else. How could I not love him? How could I even get him out of my head when he was everywhere?

Eventually, those nights of sleeping over without sex turned into nights of erotic passion.

Other nights, he would leave me at his house by myself because he had a date. However, not before running me a bath, feeding me, and kissing me goodbye. "I will be back in a few hours. You straight?" He would always ask. "I'm good," I replied. "Make sure you wrap it up," I said, laughing." You funny," said Steve" Then out the door, he went, either on a date or to hang with the fellas. During my pregnancy with my unborn daughter, I got extremely sick. The first person I called was my buddy.

Steve. "Hey Steve, what are you doing?" "Just laying here chilling, why?" what's up?" Nothing, I have the flu, in the worst way, and you can't take medication while pregnant, so I'm trying to tough it out. "Where's the ole dude at? He ain't taking care of you?" 'Yeah, right, he outside talking to

the chicken heads up the block as always. 'Call a cab and bring your ass here; I got something for you." Nah, I'm good, but thanks" "Don't make me bust your shit, get your ass over here" (that was Steve's favorite line) 'ok, I'm coming" My fever was high, and my energy was low therefore I could not get myself to look cute. I threw on a sweatsuit, called a cab, and stood outside waiting for out.

"Later," yelled Travis, watching me from up the street. Not even concerned about where I was going. I could have been on my way to the hospital; he could care less. Naturally, there were at least three bitches sitting with him. At this point, it didn't bother me; it was not about love anymore with Travis, it was about survival and security for my children. Being pregnant did not bother Steve, at least not that he ever mentioned. We never had sex during my pregnancy, and perhaps because of that, I began developing feelings for him. When I got to his house, Steve treated me like not only his best friend but also a Queen. He sponged be done occasionally to get the fever down. He gave me Tylenol and made me breakfast in bed. I could not eat, of course, but when a man gives you his bed to lie in, sits on the floor cutting up potatoes for you, and makes the full breakfast, fruit, and all, it kind of opens your eyes to what you have before you.

He was not arrogant at all. He was confident, he was sincere, and he was real, and he was confident. Yet and still with all that time we spend, He still would not make me his. Call me a fool, but even knowing, I still hoped. He had card blanch to my heart, and though many times I would tell myself to stay away from him, I could not, I would not. I was in love with a man while married to another, yet the man I loved deserved me more. Mind-body, soul, and I wanted to be there to give him just that.

Steve was building up in my heart, and this was a dangerous friendship. We understood that we were not a couple but more like best friends with benefits. This is just what we are. Yet as painful as it was, I wouldn't change a thing. I would need an intervention quick otherwise; I would live a loving life without having. What sped up the process of moving out was the reminder of how much of a dog Travis was. His mother died, and while I was carrying my unborn child of nine months, I stepped outside to see if this man had any mourning going on that he may need my shoulder to cry on. There he was, kissing another woman right in front of our house. Travis turned and looked at me with a smirk, grabbed her waist, and they walked up the road toward the funeral home. Un-freaking-believable! But then again, not really. Travis was many things, and cold and heartless was one of them. It only took thirty days after the death of my mother-in-law to plant a seed of motivation to move out, have better, and be better. With the help of my sister, I managed to get an apartment in her name. A beautiful studio, ironically in Rego Park,

Queens of all places, the same complex I met Travis in. Ironic, I'd say. It would appear life was trying to tell me something, but at that moment, I had no clue as to what that message was.

I still had my job as a cook at the county jail in Brooklyn,

Steve and I were still very much connected at every opportunity. I kept myself extremely busy to keep him out of my mind. Most people would consider our relationship a booty call; however, the only difference here was I had developed feelings for him. The only thing we never did together was share holidays like Christmas and Thanksgiving.

However, I heard from him on Valentine's Day, always got a gift, and when we were together, you would swear the way he treated me we were dating. However, we were not and not because I did not want to. He would often change the subject when it came up. Therefore, I allowed myself to be a part of this love circus in an attempt to rid myself of my loneliness and held on to faith as if it would make things change. At this moment, I have come to realize that even faith cannot deliver to you that which is not meant for you.

However, faith will remove you from where you should not be to where you ought to be. I quit my job as a cook after a brief time when I was unable to change to the day shift. Driving into work at 2 am just was not safe, and it was getting harder to find a sitter once my sitter had to quit to return to school. I was, however, able to find a job shortly thereafter. I would use my time wisely in hopes of getting Steve out of my heart.

I soon took a job at one of the most popular electronic

stores in Brooklyn, so we were always, busy and sales were great. My commission check, along with my paycheck, was sufficient for me to have a great babysitter, a furnished studio, and some fly suits and dresses. If you looked at me, you would swear I had a perfect life, my dirty little secrets of abuse, abandonment, and rape was buried deep within, although, at night, the memory of my reality was evident the moment the kids went to sleep. I could not help but cry. Constantly. I was still in a lot of pain; I just was not during it. I had my own. There was no one here to hurt me. My children now needed me, and there was no room to be weak. Eventually, I got promoted from sales to Cash Office Manager.

I made a promise to myself that they would never see hunger or worry about where they were going to sleep at night. By the grace of God, I would build a home for them despite my past.

My hours were long yet beneficial, so I would not complain. Paul was one of the older security officers who took his job profoundly serious. He was very handsome and probably around fortyish, He always wore a suit and smelled like expensive cologne. A few times, I could feel him staring at me from the corner of my eye, but I assumed he was just doing his job. I really did not take it any further than that. Hell, I had enough going on, and I was not looking for anybody.

My new position as Cash Office Manager began tonight, so there is no way I can leave yet. I made a call to Mary, my babysitter, who was so excited for me and told me to take the night. "Take the night" what do you mean? "Girl, I have watched you hustle since you moved in this building, you keep the kids clean and fed, and you have them outside every day.

You're a great mother." "I do not want to get in your business, but with all I see you do, you could use a break.

There is no school. It is Friday; celebrate or hell, go home and get some rest. You can leave them here and pick them up tomorrow; just make sure you get them by 11 am because I have errands, ok." 'Oh, Mary, thank you, but you do not have to do that." "Stop it, girl, I got you. I'm hanging up now; go live a little or sleep a lot; it's up to you." Wow, that was a beautiful thing for Mary to do. When I got off the phone, I realized all the staff had gone except for Bernard, the head of the electronics department. He always made sure things were prepared for his area for the next day. Bernard was a genius. He was moving around his area while talking with Paul. Whatever they were talking about was funny and private, for when I walked closer, they stopped talking. Both looked at me with Kool-aide smiles. "Hey, new boss lady," stated Bernard, then Paul bust out laughing. "I'm sorry, I'm sorry, I'll be nice." "Bernie, you should have been there no matter what she said; Zelda's words were like, "look, you lazy chicken head, I got your job now get to stepping!" (Referring to the old Cash Office Manager that got fired tonight, I was the new head) (Both laughing) "Hey now, be nice," I stated. "Anyway, Bernard, don't you take the F train, right/ well, could you do me a favor and wait for me, so I'm not riding by myself." However, the only thing is when you are done, you will have to clock out, is that ok?"

"I will only be about 10 minutes," I turned to Paul, and the deposit is set already for the bank, so we will be out of here quick.

Bernard opened his mouth to respond, but Paul jumped in," the only problem with that is that I'm taking Paul home tonight after we make the deposit." "Oh ok," before I can get any other words out, Paul continues, "it's Friday; I can drop you off too; it's no problem. Where do you live?" I smiled and said I live in Queens, but that is ok; I am not a party buster; I will be fine.

Plus, I don't want any trouble with your girl." Why did I say that!

The laughter in the room was addictive and loud." My girl! In what fairy tale?" Bernard almost choked; he laughed so hard. "Ok then, let us all play nice. Let me get to work; it's way too much drama."

Smiling at the two, I headed upstairs to finish, and just as I said, I was 10 minutes and done. As we pulled the gate down, we all headed to the bank to make the deposit.

Funny, I never paid Paul any mind until tonight. To see him walking tall with authority, hand on his gun, walking behind me with Bernard. I never paid any real attention, but I could smell his cologne; he wore

Obsession. I felt so protected. Hmm, no, I'm not messing with that, too much going now in my life, I thought to myself. Paul and Bernard talking as if I were not there made it easy to quickly remember my position there as an employee, not a friend. After the deposit, we headed toward the store, the train station was at the corner, and the guys were still talking. "Night, fellas," I said as I turned to wave while they were walking behind me.

"Oh, now come on, I'm not going to let you take the train. It's 11:30 at night! I don't bite," affirmed Paul, "at least not hard," laughed Bernard. "Stop before you scare the woman." "Zelda, look, let's take Bernie home, and then I will take you home; you'll be in good hands." I have nothing else to do, I thought to myself. "Ok," I agreed.

We proceeded an extra block down to Paul's car. "Nice!"

I spoke. A great dresser, good taste in cologne, and a badass car.

"Paul, can I be nosey?" Opening the door for me, replying, "Go ahead, shoot" "You work part-time at the store and yet," but before I could ask, there goes Bernie, how you got this nice stuff, man. We could not all help but laugh aloud.

I work in law enforcement as well, Zelda. 'Oh, I was just wondering," I said as I smiled at him getting into the car.

To see him walking tall with authority, hand on his gun, walking behind me with Bernard. I never paid any real attention, but I could smell his cologne; he wore Obsession.

I felt so protected. Hmm, nope, I am not messing with that, too much going now in my life, I thought to myself.) Zelda, look, let us take Bernie home, and then I will take you home; you'll be safe."

I have nothing else to do, I thought to myself. "Ok," I agreed. We proceeded an extra block down to Paul's car. "Nice!" I spoke. A great dresser, good taste in cologne, and a badass car. "Paul, can I be nosey?" Opening the door for me, replying, "Go ahead, shoot" "You work part-time at the store and yet," but before I could ask, there goes Bernie, how the hell you got this nice stuff, man. We could not all help but laugh aloud.

Marriage As The Answer

I work in law enforcement as well, Zelda. 'Oh, I was just wondering," I said as I smiled at him getting into the car.

Paul drove a black Monte with grey leather seats. I do not know the year, but it was eye candy for sure, as was he now that I had a chance to sit and talk with him. After around 20 minutes on the highway, I asked Bernard, "Where the heck do you live?"

They laughed, and Paul replied, "He lives in the Bronx." "The Bronx! Oh, so you just going to kidnap a girl and don't say anything, huh?" "No stated Paul, I said I would take you home, and I will." (Pause) right after we take Bernard home. I'd much rather have a long ride with you in the car than his motor mouth!" I could not help but laugh. "Very cute," I replied. "I'm awfully glad you have a good sense of humor, Zelda,

Forgive me?" "Yeah, I forgive you; just get me home safe, please." By the time we dropped off Bernard and made it back to Queens, it was almost two in the morning. Security was rolling the front of my building when I got out, so I felt good, and it reminded me there would be no good night kisses over here.!

"Good night, Paul, and thank you for bringing me home

safely." "Anytime," he replied. He got out of the car and opened my door.

Reaching his arms out to hug me, I allowed it. "Wow! Is this what I think it is?" I could not help it, but my mouth spoke faster than my mind could stop it. "Is that a pistol in your pocket, or are you glad to see Me.?" I smiled, and he responded by showing me his pistol on the other side of his hip on his holster, "nope, my pistol is right here." A smile was all I could do. I had not come back; I had just met my match. "Good night. Paul." "Uh-huh, that's what I thought he said. I could have interpreted that in many ways. However, I did not want to. I headed for the door and went toward the elevators, not looking back on purpose. I will say it took but two weeks of working together before I realized him watching me. Did I really want to start a relationship with all that I had going on?

I was still trying to bury the emotions that took root in my heart for Steve. I had no idea how old Paul was, but I do know he was older than I was.

Before I go any further, I must put it out there and say that I did not realize how damaged I was from all the things I had encountered up to this point. In my mind, I was over the darkness. I had two great kids, my own place, and a good-paying job to enable me to provide for them. Sure, it was a little lonely, but I did not have the worry of getting beat up, cheated on, or disrespected. What more could I need? I realize now as I write this is where we women get hemmed up.

As a defense mechanism, we tend to tell ourselves all is well.

We think if we have the basic needs for lifelike money, food, and safe shelter that we are living the good life, that we are ok.

It never dawns on us what we did or went through to get here. It gets buried in the back of our mind, and we replace it with what is before us in our efforts to forget. This we call healing ourselves. This is not healing; this is hiding. Nothing has been addressed, the pain is still there, and eventually, it gets displayed in our choices and behavior throughout our lives. We even find God. In that statement, I mean that because of our pain, we begin to go to church, pray, and shout hallelujah with excitement. The tears fall, and they fall hard; we believe we have been delivered; we are so happy that God delivered us out of the eye of the storm. Unknowing to us, we are still sitting going through. How do you wonder? We have "accepted' nothing; we have kept our nasty little secret hidden "within," and it is festering. Therefore, because we think we are free, we begin things without thinking like relationships, and then we feel so happy at the moment we label ourselves in love.

Hell, I wanted to flush Steve out of my system so badly, not because he did anything wrong, but because he did everything right and still would never be mine. I began to go to church and, like most, found peace. In reality, I have come to realize the church is nothing but a temporary band-aide for healing we don't really want to face.

In my spirit, I was lonely, as was my flesh. I was grateful for my job and a place I could call my heaven. I put my kids in private school and decided I was going to attempt to be a better parent than my mother was.

I did incredibly well ignoring the desires for Paul. I still had to face Travis when he came to get the kids. I was even good at hiding my anger and disgust that he brought his new girlfriend when Travis came to get the kids. My so-called best friend! I was not surprised at all. As long as I did not have to deal with him, and he took care of his children, so be it.

The loneliness time of being single is holiday is while the family always met at my grandmother's,' we always attended with our significant others, we as in them as I was still single. The hardest part of those holidays was that Travis was considered family, so he showed up to my grandmother's as well. He is still family; they said, family! This bastard beat me often. My dysfunctional family would gather and hug me, telling me how great I looked and how they were so proud of me. Every holiday I wanted to scream aloud, where were all of you when I needed a place to live? Sure, I understand everybody was going through things, but shit, I was on the street. Nobody ever asked about it or talked about it. However, there were always two or three family members that would corner me and tell me what havoc was raging in their homes, asking me for advice!

"Are you kidding me?"

Ok, let me get through the day; yes, I will counsel if that is what you want to call it. My grandmother always summoned me to do the grace every time as if she knew I was connected to God. I was, and it was only out of respect for God that I did the grace or counsel. This was my life, and I was not happy in it. I was dancing to everyone else's tunes. At what point will I be able to have my own music! Even working in retail has its downside. I find Paul attractive, but I do not have time to date, so I flirt innocently to feed my mind with fantasies that I can utilize while alone. My long hours leave me little time to be with the kids and during the summer there with their father. It is getting lonelier and lonelier. The loneliness got louder, and no matter how much a mommy I played or counseled to the friends and strangers that came in my path. I purposely continued to distance myself from

Steve; it was hurting not to be his girlfriend. More so because I could not understand why, since he is now single, I could not shut it off. I decided to see if there was anything worth developing by dating Paul. I managed to go against my better judgment, and I made up in my mind that I would ask Paul out for dinner! I planned it strategically. I went to my favorite clothing store the day before and purchased a very snazzy low back spaghetti strap slinky, yet not to slutty blue dress from the David Benjamin Collection. My closet was filled with his suits.

They were business-style yet sexy at the same time.

When I wore them, it said, powerful mind, body, and soul. Nothing less than that would define me. At least not in my opinion.

We were about to close, and Mr. Felder was still here, which meant I did not have to make the deposit. I made my way towards the front door where Paul stood looking his usual handsome self. I still do not know how old he was, but it didn't matter; I just wanted the company, and truth be told, it was over a year since I had been touched, and well, you understand.

Paul, I said, in my most flirtatious tone, how Many hearts are you on your way to break tonight?"

Laughing in surprise, Paul replied, uh, maybe yours, why"? Ouch, he was as quick as I was.

Well, I have a free night away from the little ones and was just wondering if I could have the pleasure of taking you to dinner? You up for some company? 'It would be my pleasure, he said. Giving him my famous, slight head tilt and eyes up with that come hither look, I said, "great; I will meet you at your car when you get off."

Felder is locking up, so I am off already.

How is that?

"No, that's not cool. Why don't you come back and meet me in the front of the store when I lock up and walk with me to my car" I got nothing to hide. I am single. I realized that I had never even thought about if he was dating or not.

"Sounds like a plan. See you soon." I headed out of the store to occupy the 45 minutes I had left.

As I was approaching the store, I noticed there was a short heavyset woman standing outside, and she appeared to be heartbroken while apparently pleading to Paul. Hmm, I thought to myself, what is that all about, and do I really want to know? He said he was single, but evidently, she is not aware of that status.

I boldly walked toward the entrance to go into the store; I was not going to say anything when I passed them to avoid drama. Just as I was approaching, Paul looked up and said, "I will be ready in a moment, ok, hon." Oh my goodness. I did not want to be in whatever this was. I heard her say, "that's why I can't have you back? What about us. At this point, I was really regretting the invitation. I had extended everything in me told me to produce an excuse and go home. It was not five minutes before Paul came back in the store, just as Felder was coming down the stairs with the deposit. I'm ready, Paul; Paul clicks the lights while waiting for him to lock up. Felder just had to go there.

"Zelda, I thought you left already" Nope, still here, was all I said and was all I was going to say. I walked beside Felder so Security could do his job and walk behind us; gun displayed and ready for anything.

Felder made the drop and was off to his car parked across the street from the bank. Night guys, he uttered in a tone that said," I wonder what you two are up to. Night, see you Saturday (I was off tomorrow and happy for that). I pride myself on being a woman of class. There was a restaurant I had seen every day but never had the nerve to go into. It faces the Brooklyn Bridge, and the seating faces the water and the city. It goes around like a merry-go-round, and I found it to be the most romantic spot in Brooklyn. Parkers Lighthouse. Exquisite and popular amongst those who have success.

I did not have success, but I would position myself there, and perhaps the Gods would be merciful one day.

108

We got to the restaurant, and although we didn't really have to drive far, it was long enough for Paul to demonstrate his great taste in music and his power Boss speaker system. His car still had that new smell. This was a divine and romantic evening that I allowed myself to have without sex.

Just build a friendship and see if it will go anywhere. During the holidays, the store is always packed; then, towards closing, you can hear a pin drop. This day, my mind went on a frenzy of its own. I found myself staring to the point that when Paul saw me, I locked my eyes on him to say I was interested. There was no one watching, so I made my move.

"Paul, would you escort me to my office please?" "Sure," he replied.

As we walked up the stairs, I could feel him watching my ass, which I purposely made sway in an alluring way. I turned around and looked right at him to let him know, I knew he was watching, and yes, he could have it if he so desired. We got to my office, and Paul opened the door. I walked in and motioned for him to come in, and he complied willingly. I reached across him when he got in and closed the door and turned the lock.

Never taking my eyes off his, I moved in closer. Placing my hands on his cheek, I moved in slowly, passionately. His tongue was warm and flavorful, and mine, well, mine was hungry and hot. Kissing him, I decided that this moment was about me. Taking his right hand, I guided it up under my dress. Wearing only Channel #5 underneath, I placed his hands right on my pussy, and he was a man who needed no instruction. His hands were large, as were his fingers. Brown and thick, slowly parting my lips and inserting his index finger in a slow in and out motion. I lifted my leg and placed it on my desk to allow room to feel him finger fuck me. My pussy was so wet, so hungry. It had been so long, and he began to kiss my neck, slowly working his way to my breast. My nipples were standing out in need of attention. "Oh my God, I need this right now," I whispered. I allowed my pussy to enjoy his presence, and it was intriguing that no one knew what was going on behind closed doors.

In my selfishness, I pulled back so that his finger came out. Staring at him, I undid his pants; not even concerned about a condom at the moment, I pulled his pants down slowly to his ankles, and I lowered my body with it. Catching a hint of the fragrance on his member, I paused for the cause and began to lick his member in a sensuous rhythm, enjoying his soft moans. Standing up slowly, I sat him in the chair and mounted him in a teasing fashion. Slow up and down, tightening up on the inside. His hands were stroking my hair, our eyes meeting every so often, and the kisses, oh, they tasted like strawberry now or later candy. A candy he always eats.

It seemed like we had been at it forever; he could really hold it down. I was about to come, and when he realized that I was at my peak, he cupped my breast in his hands and did this fast stroke with his tongue across my nipples. The explosion was well past due. It was when I felt him grabbing my hair hard that I realized he, too, was coming.

That is when it hit me. "Shit, we weren't using protection.

"AH SHIT IT," I said in a low whisper. "Let it go," he did, and it was beautiful, powerful, and necessary. When it was over, we quickly pulled ourselves back in order, and he kissed my eyes and said," I see you." "I'm going to stay here for a while," blushing. "I think you should," Paul replied.

He was smiling and leaving my office. "Have a great day" "I have one already he said and walked away. What did

I just do. I thought to myself. "You know what, Zee, let it flow;" stop analyzing, "I said aloud to myself.

"Enjoy, for a moment without analyzing" I took a deep breath and did just that.

During one of our romantic interludes at the Holiday Inn. The conversation about relationships came up. Strategically, of course.

Come to find out; Paul was divorced for six years before

we met and sober three years thus far. He had a girlfriend that they had just broken up with since she was still into alcohol and drugs, and he had changed his life around. Therefore, that was what that little scene was in front of the store a few months ago was all about; she wanted a second chance.

At this moment, I was turned on by what I thought was loyalty. As per Paul, he stated once he breaks up with someone, he does not stay connected. This, as he says, includes his ex-wife and six children. Right here proves my point that we all are given advice from the creator, yet we allow our circumstances to override our common sense.

If Paul wasn't willing to be in his children's lives, what makes me think he would be a suitable, let alone a responsible mate? However, the loneliness was loud. I wanted to feel I meant something to someone. Since Travis despised me and had hand issues and Steve did not want me, I had a hidden hope that Paul would be my happily ever after.

Do not judge me; you have done the same thing many times. Think about it. Now that we got that out the way let us continue.

I was right in believing Paul was my Mr. Right, right now, he was faithful, took excellent care of me, and worked seven days a week. I never wondered or questioned him, as he never gave me a reason to.

Two years had passed, and Paul had asked me to marry him and move in with him. Well, he gave me a stuffed teddy bear with a ring tied to the bow. He never once said marry me. I looked at the ring with such excitement and simply said yes. I did not think twice. I packed up my children and moved into his apartment. The sex of an older man was unique, as was I, and there was nothing left for me to hurt from. I simply stayed out of contact with Steve and built a life with Paul. Steve, however, never left the back of my mind.

My life with Paul was great, yet when he eventually realized that our nineteen-year age difference was starting to show.

There was so much I did not know about the "grown-up world" after all, I was only twenty years old. During one of our romance days created by yours truly, Paul played a song for me 'Love Under New Management" At this moment, I allowed myself to be vulnerable and tell him all about my life my whole life how my mother made me move in with a man seven years older than me, how she abandoned me, and how I lived on the street. Yet no matter how hard I tried; I could not get myself to tell him I had been raped twice. The shame was too deep, and I did not want to face it.

Paul's compassion was felt in the embrace he gave as he utters," I will never hurt you, and you do not ever have to worry about me leaving you. Boom! That was it; he was my mister right, who could do no wrong.

We had the perfect wedding; I was the beautiful black Cinderella draped in a shimmering white gown with an eight-foot-long veil, and to introduce me were with seven stunning brides' maids draped in cream that complimented their fabulous shape, accessorized with cream satin long-armed gloves, and each girl carried a single tall, stemmed Lilly.

My knight in shining armor wore a black tuxedo with tails and, to compliment him, an African color cummerbund. His ushers, all seven of them, wore the same. We stopped traffic and turned the heads of all who looked upon us. There was nothing more beautiful to see on that deceitful day. Ladies do not ever put your guards down simply because of sweet words; when you know in the back of your mind, he, or she, for some, have already displayed signs that something is not quite right. For example, two weeks before this beautiful yet deceitful event, Paul and I had an argument. Since I discovered that he had regained communication with his children, I felt, why wouldn't you invite them? He could give no valid reason. Oh, and by the way, I only knew he had been communicating with them because I found a piece of paper with his ex-wife's name on it as well as the discovery that he had often been contacting as per the cell phone bill.

Paul's explanation was that he wanted to fix his relationship with his children, and I believed him. Far be it for me to interfere with something like that. So why then was my question would you not invite them?

As it turned out, they knew nothing about me. I had asked

God to show me the truth in this matter by having the Pastor who was scheduled to do our pre-marriage counsel does not show up on the day of our appointment. He did not, yet once again, I put that off as coincidence as opposed to not hearing the voice of God when he was answering my prayer.
Passion can also make you lose sight of your vision as well.

We had numerous nights of romance that I created. In my mind, I was creating a haven for him that he never had, so what reason would he ever have to cheat on me. Paul came home to endless nights of satin sheets spread on the floor with a cheese basket, white wine, and the penetrating sounds of Barry White, Al Jarreau, and Baby Face. I was always in something different. from colors to styles, lace, satin, cotton.

One night Paul came home, and it was Valentine's Day;

I was wrapped in a red bow. My makeup was always flawless. I purposely woke with the sun before him to shower, do my hair, and apply my makeup, then return to bed so that when he woke, I was as beautiful as I was when I went to sleep. Part of my creativity was little notes of instruction on the door or flower petals that led to the bedroom.

A videotape of my wet body singing to him in the shower. Polaroids of various half nudies, with little I, love you quotes that led to the bedroom door that said enter at your own risk. I was not a big reader, so these things came from my own desires. The sex was phenomenal, say the least (or at least I thought so at the time). You would think that with all that plus cooking cleaning all the way down to ironing his underwear! In no way would I have thought this awesome man of mine would be having an affair over the entire duration of a six-year relationship with his ex-wife. Our relationship was so perfect, but in the back of my mind, something was not right. Whatever that something was, I really did not want to know. I loved my life with Paul, and I really did not want it to change.

What was that something that was not right? Well, I discovered while driving on my way home from work, there was a car parked at the corner that looked familiar.

It was Paul. What was Paul doing on this side of town?

He said he was working overnight again. He was not in the car, so I called him. He did not pick up. I literally called him eight times, and he did not pick up! I paged him, how many times I do not know, but he never responded. 'Oh no, this was not happening'! Not my knight in shining armor! I pulled up to the corner enough to still have his car in my rear-view mirror, and I waited to see what would unfold. I called his job and was told he is on vacation this week! What the shit? Are you serious? My heart pounded so hard it hurt.

I went through a whole pack of Newport's before I realized the sun was starting to come up.

Then there it was, Paul was coming from around the corner with a woman and a duffle bag!

Son of a Bitch! What the hell? As I watched him open his trunk and put the bag into the car, he stepped around to open the door for her; I picked up my phone and called him. He closed her door, and as he walked, he picked up the phone. "Hey, how are you"? "How am I? I yelled,

"I've been calling you all night."

"Well, babe, you know I can't answer the phone at work."

"You ok," he asked. This fool did not see me and was talking like everything was ok. I'm good, just a little lonely. Well soon as my relief comes in. I can clock out, but I need to stop at my mother's house first. I should be home by the afternoon.

"Ok," I said, as calm as I could. I hung up the phone, and the first thought in my mind was to rear his ass. I did a quick

U-turn and raced towards his car and pulled up to the side of him.

His head was looking down, and she and I met eye to eye. I pulled my car in front of him, and the son of a bitch took off like a bat out of hell. I raced behind him as if he owed me money.

One thing I can say is men do not think it worth a dam. Paul had since purchased another car. A white sports car. He pulled into a block and parked as if this white car was not going to stand out! Wow, he really was a piece of work. As I pulled in the block, he turned off his car, and I got out, as did he, quickly. Fear all over his face and unsure of what I was going to do next. "What the hell is going on here? I yelled to him. His lame reply was, I was just dropping Dee off at her house" I ran into her on my way to my car." "You mother fucking bastard"! Without thinking, my hands began to swing as if my life depended on it. I was crushed. I slapped him in his face and left in my car, but not before scratching up the passenger side of his car with a piece of glass I picked up from the ground. It made no sense in my mind what little I could muster at the time to curse her out. I married him, not her. But there will still be hell to pay if he is foolish enough to come home.

Ironically, he made it home before I did! I laugh when I think of that. The baby sister was there about to leave as I walked into the house. She knew something was up, and she left fast enough as if to not have to be witness to it. When we hear of these types of scenes, we always say what we would do. But the truth is you never know what you are

going to do until it's you.

The first thing I noticed was that Paul was sweating profusely. I had plenty of time to cry and think on my way home.

Now here we are face to face; Paul is waiting for the "big fight" I am not going to give it to him. I kissed the kids and began talking about their day as if nothing had happened. Paul went into the bedroom, and as the kids were changing clothes, I walked into our so-called heaven where all things sexual, were no holds barred used to be and noticed his duffel bag on the bed and made my way to it. He was standing by the bathroom and not fast enough to stop me from opening the bag. Condoms, there you have it. No words need to be said. I lifted the box, and as I looked down, I noticed a vibrator made for women and edible underwear. The same kind he bought me a few months ago. "Just because," he said. This was it; it was over. I went and tucked in the kids and got in my bed, alone. There will be no sleeping on the couch, no screaming or yelling or fighting. I will find peace within my pain.

Some way. As I lay there, I was amused that Paul just sat at the edge of the bed with the TV on as if afraid to lay beside me. Smart man. I lay there fighting successfully to hold back my tears and refrain from speaking. Reflecting on our very first date. I should have kept my mouth closed. That day was as clear as this one. Apparently, Paul had been interacting on a day-to-day basis with his ex before we met and continued after that. I would not have been to upset with that since they have children. Why lie? I could not handle that devastation. I put my walls down and allowed myself to be vulnerable to a man who didn't respect me enough to be as honest to me as I was to him. Paul produced the nerve to try to discuss what had happened, and I obliged him. I wanted to know. I had to know. Why? I don't know. Yet finding out she had been at dances we gave and functions from the job just burned me up. There were many nights he confessed to but always tried to find an excuse for it. "She was at my mother's house," "I ran into her with my daughter." Paul's excuse list was long and seeped of bullshit. Come to find out, she lived in the same building as his mother, and I had seen her many times when she nodded hello. I just never knew who she was. To me, it says you do not deserve my loyalty. For years, I had been lied to. I gave him a son eight years into the marriage, she had seen him, spent time with both, and I was the fool on the outside unaware. It is this kind of humiliation that makes a woman seek revenge. Oh yes, you had better believe I was plotting. I now have three children from two marriages; I do not know where my parents are and my family, although in my life, well, I still don't feel complete. In fact, I feel very insignificant. To say the least. I had taken the test for officer two years ago, and finally that call from The Department of Corrections cam. I was so excited and scared at the same time. The academy challenged me, and I had much to prove to myself. My new job as an officer would assume a lot of my time, and in my mind, since Paul loved our son and his ex-wife more than me, I would take any overtime I could get. I felt important. The numbers on my paycheck also made me tough it out as well. Still angry and still married to Paul. Paul ended up having three other affairs since our little ex-wife moment. I find it confusing now and even then. Why do men feel the need to lie to another? With all that, we do as women to make them feel like Kings. In the end, we become the peasant. Like many women, I stayed in my marriage; part of me still desired love, and I would live this false life for now. However, working in law enforcement at this point, there is a lot to do and many people to associate with. Our payday fell on Thursdays, and that is the night most officers would go to the local bar and socialize and let our hair down. I began to look forward to this day, as no one there knew what I was going thru so much and was in so much pain.

I stopped worrying about what Paul was doing or whom he was with. He was not home half the time anyway. However, every so often, I would find myself attempting to talk about our so-called marriage, telling him what I needed, asking him if he wanted to be with me. His reply was always yes, and that he was so sorry that he had caused me so much pain. Eventually, like most of you, my guards came down unintentionally. I did not want to fool around, yet it had been almost a year, and we still were not having sex. 'It's not you, it's me," he would always tell me. One night I decided I would challenge him.

In my best nighty from Victoria Secrets, I walked into the room as he was lying down listening to slow jams. I stood in front of him and stared deep into his eyes. "I want you," kneeling toward him to kiss him, his face became distorted, a look of disgust! "What the heck is your problem?" I yelled, "If you don't want me to say so, but I can't live like this anymore" "I won't live like this anymore. "This is the 9th or 10th time we are having this problem, and nothing is changing. Whatever changes that do take place don't last long" 'Why do you always add a number of how many times we've talked or how many times you tried to come at me with sex?" He asked. "Come at you!" I yelled. I'm your wife Paul!" "Know this, if you begin to notice I'm not at home and I am smiling even though you're not treating me like I'm yours, note that you've just been officially warned!" "I want you to remember how many times your wife confronted you with her needs, and you ignored them." "You feel me now!" "I am telling you to your damn face that you are neglecting me as your wife, and I am not happy, and I am not satisfied"! "Take me or leave me the hell alone!" There it is in black and white. I told him what I needed, asked if he could give it, offered him a divorce if he was not happy, yet he never took me up on it.

Paul was always willing to work it out, as he says. Paul sat up and pulled me to him. "I'm sorry, I just got a lot on my mind, I haven't been feeling sexual, and I guess perhaps I am taking it out on you." Forgive me" I love you and I want this to work."

The attention lasted for four months, and then we were right back where we started. I was through.

"This is the 17th time I am coming to you, and I want a divorce; I am not happy, I am horny, and apparently, you could care less". "You said it was you, not me, and yet whatever it is with you, you haven't fixed." I'm done."

"I don't want a divorce; I want my family," said Paul.

Bullshit was the term that came to my mind. I was too foolish at the time to realize that since we both had a decent job that it was cheaper to keep her, and that is what he was doing. Fine, I will play that game.

You do not want to touch me; someone else will. That was my final thought. (Phone ringing)

"Who is calling me at this time of night" I wondered. "Hello" "Hey Zee, it's Victoria; the girls and I are going to the club tonight; you want to join us?" "Tonight?" "Why you ain't call me yesterday, I got nothing to wear, and my hair is a mess" Victoria was no one of those women who does not let up easily. "Girl, please, pull out one of your black minis and pull out the hot curler; you got plenty of time." "We're not leaving till 11:30 tonight; it's only 9 pm" tonight, my cousins and sisters would make it a girl's night—something I really needed.

And yes, despite my childhood, we were close. When I was married to Travis, it seemed we were all going through something. So, I created a group called the Ng's, and it was short for Ninety's Girls. The group consisted of myself, my sister Dana and four of my cousins, Carol, Tammy, Lisa, and Pam. We would meet every second Saturday; we would share out drama, and I would give advice. It really built an empowering circle.

The truth was, many of them had no idea what I was

going through or had been through, for that matter. Perhaps I should have talked to them instead of being angry. I can admit that. In any event, we partied like rock stars on the weekends, but not before I put my children to bed. They never knew mommy was not home and a babysitter was there. Leave when they fall asleep and be back before they awoke; that was my life. Paul came and went. Mostly went.

Defining Love

Saturday Nights, at the Proper Night Club in Queens, that night was set aside for just us girls, and that was our spot. We went because my uncle was also the picture man, and he was good at what he did. Well-known and well-loved. He was like my second father, always there for me, full of wisdom. I loved him dearly.

In any event, the girls and I were sharp as always. Sexy and classy, and we waited for no man to ask us to dance.

We danced on our own or together.

This Saturday, December 2004, would change my life

forever. I would discover what it was like to have someone really care about you and appreciate you. It would also be the year when I first experienced the feeling of losing a child before it had a chance to see life outside my womb. We walked through the doors picked out our table to sit for the night. Glancing around, seeking possible prospects. Yes, I was feeling frisky, I had not planned to have sex with anyone, and I just wanted to flirt. Feel special. Fill the void that was so deep inside me.

To my left, a group of couples, nothing happening there; one thing I would never do is play with a toy that doesn't belong to me. In the center of the dance floor, I realized how crowded it was. A lot of single women as well. Black spandex all over the entire place; ironically, I was the only one there in white spandex; naturally and unintentionally, I stood out to the brothers by the bar.

The television hanging for those who wanted to watch the game was to the right. And sure, enough one man was watching it too. A Heineken stood in front of him, and he seemed unimpressed by the women there. He never even glanced at the dance floor. Have you ever had one of those friends that have the kind of head that you could spot even if they were not facing you?

Well, I noticed a former co-worker; I knew exactly who

he was. On the job, I never paid him any attention; I had too much going on.

That didn't mean I would have to be rude, so I made myself walk over to simply say hello. He asked who I was with and where was I sitting. After I told him, he sorts of dismissed me!

Well, alright, laughing to myself, let me go back to my table. His name was Chuck. Ladies, when I tell you he was something to look at, I don't mean his actual body, something about his eyes alone; if you stopped and paid attention, they spoke whatever words you needed to hear. Bass in his voice, his skin was light, smooth, and muscular.

His name boldly tattooed on his arm" CHUCK," Somewhat Bo legged, or at least it appeared to be, and the ass of a King. He was very forward, so much it was dam near erotic.

I caught myself feeling quite tingly as I sat talking to the girls at the table the night we met. Was it because he dismissed me? Yes, but I took it as he wasn't after a piece of ass just to relax and watch the game, and that's precisely what he was doing. Believe me when I tell you there were enough women in the club that no man would have been alone unless he wanted to be. In my mind, he is coming over to say hello and introducing himself to my girlfriends displayed a level of genuine concern or interest in talking to me or one of the girls anyway. He spoke firmly in his greeting to all the ladies with me, Carol, Tammy, Danielle, Lisa, and Pam all seemed to have had a soft gasp when he spoke. It was the funniest thing to witness. Pam was the most outspoken. Damn, is it me, or is everybody hearing

Barry White's voice at this table?" We all laughed, and as the DJ started his selection of music, I was ready to dance.

"You ladies want something to drink? "Ah shit, a polite

Barry White, Jazz, if you don't want him, can I have him? Hey, wait, Chuck, do you (in her Barry White impersonation voice) practice what you preach? "Yes," and he walked away to get our drinks. There wasn't a dry eye at the table when Chuck walked away; it was too funny to stay silent.

I was ready to dance, so I told Lisa to watch my bag, and since Chuck was still online, I had a chance to get out and shake my thing. 'Ting a ling a ling, bounce back and swing" aw, that was my jam! My hips had a mind of thereon, and it took me to a place where I was free. I was not hurting in my heart; I was happy and still standing. Music was my lover, and I danced passionately. I was not thinking about anyone, not the men there, not Paul, not even Chuck. I was so in love with myself when I was on the dance floor. The music hypnotized my mind; I was no longer in this world.

The trance was broken the moment he changed the tune to LL Cool J' Doing it well, and everywoman was now on the dance floor. My girls were walking my way, and I saw Chuck standing by our table talking to a few fellas. I locked eyes on Chuck and then reminded myself that I was not here for that. The girls and I were tearing it up. In sync,

I want to call you big daddy and scream your name, ah yes, I was feeling this, and my body was starting to react, so I continued dancing with my eyes close; the next thing I knew, Chuck was in front of me in step. No talking, we locked eyes, and by the time we realized we had just danced four songs straight and were the only ones on the floor. "I see you can keep up," I stated flirtatiously. 'You better watch it, girl; I'm going to send you home," Chuck replied. (His favorite line) We laughed, and I decided to let me go back to my seat, this man was turning me on, and he didn't even know it. Keep in mind it was not in my intention to pick anyone up flirt with anybody, let alone be provocative. Can I blame it on the alcohol, as Jamie Foxx says? Not really, because through all of this, I still hadn't had my drink yet. Chuck and I both went to our corners, so to speak, and continued our planned-out night, Him watching the sports channel me chatting and laughing with the girls.

Leave it to Pam, So Jazz, you haven't been fucked in a

year, and you still married to that son of a bitch, now you got this fine brother here who apparently can keep up with your ass. Question, why the hell are you still at this table?

Lisa couldn't help but spit out her drink during her laughter thank goodness the rest of the girls held their liquor in.

"She's right said Lisa, I saw that bulge in his pants, and if I was you, I sure wouldn't be sitting with any females. I wouldn't give a dam if I did come with yawl.

The women at another table heard her, and everyone was cracking up. I tried to appear calm, cool, and collective.

They don't know my pain, so they won't understand my reaction. Believe me, I was slowly losing control, and my body was responding in ways I could not control. By 4 am, we were all ready to go since the club was also closing.

Inez was getting prepared to call a cab when Pam blurted hey

Chuck are you going to be a gentleman and drive us home. "My car is too small for all yawl," he replied. Chuck decided he would wait with us until the cab came; he put his hands around me in response to the others saying it was cold. Personally, I was warm, sure I was dressed sexy, but I had sense enough to be warm when I left my house. The moment Chuck put his arms around me was the most peaceful feeling I had ever encountered. It wasn't sexual at all; it felt safe. Thick arms, my head buried in his neck, and if I stood any closer, I would be inside him. Oh, how I wish. Thinking back now gives me Goosebumps. But I won't say too much of that at this moment. I couldn't help but ask," what kind of car do you drive?"

He pointed to a small four-door at the corner. That could fit us. What don't you like, my friends? I said, laughing, "No, I just have a lot of stuff in there.

I am a man that believes in staying prepared for anything. He was right; he had everything and anything in his car. It wasn't messy, just full. Like the gentlemen he is, Chuck told Lisa, tell your girl to cancel the cab, give me a moment to clear out my car, and I will drive you home. Ahhh! How sweet, I said to him, kissing his cheek. The ride was a mere 20 minutes by highway, and as the girls got out of the car. I took a moment to say thank you. I don't recall who gave up the number first, but what's more important was that we exchanged them. Chuck motioned his finger toward his lips, instructing me to kiss him. I've always been good at following instructions. This kiss would tell exactly how my body was feeling. It was gentle, deep, sensuous, and warm.

Most importantly, it was long. He was lost for words, which is a great sign. I got out of the car and waved goodbye. The girls and I all lived in the same building on different floors.

By the time I got to the 12th floor, I was floating to the point that I didn't notice that when I got off the elevator, there stood Paul, on the phone, trying to function as if it was a guy on the other end. Apparently, she doesn't know sound travels, I uttered as I walked towards our apartment. The kids were gone for the holiday. Perfect time for me to indulge without being interrupted in tonight's events. I ran the water and poured my peach bubble bath. Pour me some Beranger's White Zinfandels and life a few frankincense mixed with opium oils scones. The scene was so serene it was a dam shame I was alone. I heard Paul go into the bedroom still on the phone. I put on my cd player, and it was me, Toni Braxton, and Chuck.

The first selection was "Candlelight" sensuality; here I come, it was my time, and I made love to Chuck in my mind while in that tub. My nipples were so erect, and while parts of me felt somewhat guilty, the other part of me, the hungry, lonely, humiliating part, didn't give a shit. "Just enjoy, baby. You deserve this moment and so much more," I told myself.

This was the first time I had allowed my body to turn on.

Paul and I slept in the same bed but never touched, and that was fine because I didn't want him. In my mind, I would keep tonight's kiss in a tiny box and pull it out to create a world where I was wanted, even if it was by myself. Chuck made it a habit to call me daily, for no particular reason, just to say, "Hi, how you doing? You, ok? Ok, cool, talk to you later."

Chuck had asked me to spend New Year's Eve with him! We know that ole saying whomever you spend New Year's with is who you spend the year with! I was excited. Overly excited. Paul had no clue the imprint he left on me.

I don't know how he did; I just know that even now, almost a decade later, as I write, my smile is all over my face. I almost canceled our date. Simply because I was having so much fun, I was falling, and I did not know why. What was it that made me tremble at the sound of his name, smile at the thought of his face, relax without my guards up in his embrace, and have orgasms when I allowed myself to go into la-la land thinking about him? Perhaps this is not a good thing, but it felt so dam good.

He was unattached and wanted to share New Year with me! Whatever it is we're sharing is flowing naturally. 11:50 pm, just ten minutes before 2005, I had to ask him; I had to be certain. Sitting in his van that also had everything he needed, and he called that van Big Blue. Here we go,

I'm going to put it out there, and wherever it falls, it falls. I have a question for you I said nervously" shoot he replied and sat up straight as if he was ready for anything that came out my mouth. I proceeded. If we are going to do this, I need to know exactly what this is. Are you in this for the sex? If so, be honest and give me the option to decide if that's what I want to do? Or are you in this to see to hang around and see if this is going to turn into a relationship?

He looked right into my eyes and locked in on them. Taking what seemed like forever, although silently I was glad, he was thinking about it. "Yeah, yes, I want to stick around and see where this is going to go. WOW! I felt so happy inside but tried to remain as confident as possible. 11:58 pm was here; Chuck moved closer took my hands and said, let's pray the year out! My heart was populating, not that I had a fear of praying, but because he was a praying man and the fact that it was important to me. That was also first on my wish list in a relationship.

Which I disregarded when I found out that Paul was not a praying man or a church-going man for that.

Like I said in the beginning, "we always get a message from God but are we listening. No? We seek our own ways to heal. Chuck didn't know it in hindsight, I wish I would have told him face to face, but at that moment, he had my heart. For reasons hard to put into words. We hadn't even had sex yet.

But boy was I wanted to; we just hadn't gotten there yet.

Midnight is here, and what we're we are doing at that very second kissing. Lips locked hearts and mind clear, no games, here. I was content. So much that Steve became a thing way in the back of my mind. A great friend I will always cherish but will never have my heart nor make me his own, and I was fine with this. For Steve was not a praying man either, if he was, it never showed, but I take no credit from him; he is a great friend that I will cherish forever.

It was all about Chuck, I still hung out with the girls from time to time, and even on the dance floor, no man could penetrate the barrier I had around me. When I go in, I go in deep and sincere. No one can call me a cheater for any moment that one had my body. It was clear that no one else had it for a long time prior.

After a long weekend with Chuck at Atlantic City, someplace we also had in common and didn't feel the need to stick up underneath each other while there. We were together and didn't have to be together, and I never worried about that.

Well, when I got home, there was Paul, a sickening sight to my eyes. Where were you? Excuse me? Uh, I owe you no explanation you answer to your ex-wife or whomever you are sleeping with; you don't have any rights left over here. I made it clear months ago I wanted a divorce, so what's your problem.

"I'm moving out he said, I signed my lease last week" Angered only because I didn't know ahead of time, but I have a good job, so I am not worried. 'I paid for the next two months of rent for you, but I am taking the car. We both had one. Taking my car? Why? You have one, and you'd leave me without transportation? You can take the bus, he replied' fine, I replied, angered, and pissed at the same time.

That week was the longest week in my life; my uncle had gotten sick, extremely sick. Chuck went with me to visit him, and not surprisingly, he knew my uncle as well. My uncle is a very straightforward man who speaks with diplomacy. A lesson he tried to teach me. I'm still learning. In any event, Chuck walked over to shake his hand, and uncle asked him, "Hey man, you seeing my niece, or you guys' just friends.? I'm seeing her; once again, that beautiful feeling of being wanted to embrace me. Well, I need to know you going to take care of her? Are you going to take care of her? She's my favorite niece? (To my uncle, we were all his favorite niece, each for a special reason, my sister

for her peas and rice, me for keeping family together and playing referee. Always available if I can be. Wild yet still a praying woman is what he said I was, assuring me it was no fault of my own)

136

I will take incredibly good care of her; Chuck replied and gave me that sexy smile.

Never knew love like this

That night I went home to an empty home with Chuck at my side; my bed welcomed him. I welcomed him. I wanted to confide in him and tell him how nervous I was because it had been so long. But no words were needed. He was so gentle; it lay here in my black thongs braless, nipples erected because I was afraid.

I turned on my favorite cd, Mariah Carey's "We Belong Together," then proceeded to sit on the bed and watched him take off his clothes; no words were said, and then again, it wasn't needed. He stood there for a moment admiring me, slightly smiling. He had the most beautiful body I'd ever seen. I don't know which was more enticing, the cut in his arms, his chest, the masculinity that stood firm in his legs and posture, or his lips, which he had a way perching together.

My goodness, he was handsome, sexy, all those things you hope for. His body was crème de la crème. At that very moment, I caught feelings of what, I am not sure, but it was taking me over, and I was trying so hard to keep my emotions in check.

To appear as if I was in control, I laid as if it was all good.

In my mind, all I could think of was what if I didn't satisfy him. It had been so long. Slowly, Chuck approached me on the bed. He was so gentle, and yes, so huge, I must put it out there. His eyes never left mine, even when he penetrated, and when he did close his eyes, it was only for a second, during his climaxing moment, and even then, he managed to raise his head and looked me straight in my eyes. I wanted to inhale him and keep him in me if that were at all possible.

We had daily communication and saw each other frequently. Life was finally paying off. I still had a good job; I was paying my rent, and Paul had agreed to continue paying the rent until the divorce was final. It's been four months since he left, and I am loving it. In the back of my mind, I was working on my divorce. I was trying to be ready in case he wanted me to be his Mrs. Horn. I was ready to do be anything and everything for Chuck.

The one thing I realize today that I didn't realize there was I should have taken time to really "know" him. Sure, we talk, but what are we talking about. These answers play a huge part in a relationship; even more so do the questions.

But I didn't want to rock the boat, I was happy, and I wanted to keep him, so to speak. A few months later, I was late on my period, and I was petrified! My tubes are tied, and this should not be one of my problems. What am I going to tell him? Shit, I don't want a relationship that's going to be based on a forced responsibility. I couldn't tell the girls, or rather, I didn't want to tell them to avoid having to hear why I didn't make him wear a condom. Why I thought to myself. I'm not doing anything with anyone, I get checked yearly, and hell, we saw each other almost every day, if not every other day, so where did he have time?

Chuck was coming by in a few hours today; we're going to one of his favorite Mexican Restaurants. I have to tell him there is no getting around it.

Chuck' I missed my visitor" There I said it. Not too bad.

"Your visitor? What are you talking about? Dam, ok, here it is, I think I'm pregnant, I'm sorry' holding back my tears expecting some sharp mean response. 'Well, ok, if you are, we just take care of it" Take care of it? What did he say, my mind jumping to conclusions, "yes, I'll be here, we take care of him or her together and do what we need to do? That statement could have meant anything, but at least it didn't mean abortion, which I am strictly against.

Well, we got that out the way and headed for the restaurant.

"Senor! Key Paso, you finally come with a friend, huh? The host is familiar with Chuck, and apparently, he comes alone, so once again, Chuck's actions continue to make me feel special.

A few weeks have passed, and my period is still missing in action. I decided that it was time to go to the doctors and see what was going on. Positive! I'm with child. I'm not sure how to feel at the moment. Happy, sad, nervous, scared, so many emotions. The doctor said I was only seven weeks and asked me if I wanted to discuss an alternative. I was told I was lucky that it was not ectopic as most women who become pregnant after a tubal ligation normally get pregnant in their tubes. There was no alternative. Chuck and I have a child coming into the world, and we will just take it one day at a time. I didn't want to tell him yet.

He hadn't mentioned it either.

In the back of my mind, I wanted to set the perfect stage. I would plan a perfect romantic night and tell him. I found myself looking in the baby department one day at the Queens Center Mall. Happiness never felt this good.

Love was giving me another chance. I went into the Hallmark store and found the perfect card that said, "You're about to be a daddy… again." It was the cutest little yellow card with ducks and little cars and dolls. I purchased it and decided I would go back down to The Children's Place, the very same store where I bought all my children's clothing and accessories. There, a blanket lay spread out on display, pink, blue, and white, perfect for either gender. Excited, I walked towards the steps, and in the middle of my excitement, I was watching a woman with a child, her belly stuck far out. It was obvious she was going into labor soon. Her husband was holding her hand, and such happiness surrounded them. In watching them, I missed a few steps and fell down every step in that stairwell all the way to the bottom.

Panic hit some, while others chuckled. An older man and a few people rushed to help me stand up. Security found her way to me and asked if I wanted to go to the hospital. I felt fine. I'll be ok. Of course, I changed my mind about buying that blanket and decided I better take my butt home.

No sooner than I got to the main exit, it happened, a sharp, piercing pain from my belly to my vagina. I doubled over and tried to move out of people's way, and I could feel warm liquid flowing down my legs, and my crème-colored denim jeans were saturated in blood! No! This can't be happening. How could I have been so stupid? Why didn't I watch where I was going? The nearest hospital was less than five minutes away.

Security had seen me and had already called 911. They arrived faster before I knew it. There were cutting my jeans to see where the blood was coming from. The verdict was easily determined; I was losing my baby! The joy that came into my life was leaving before I had a chance to enjoy its presence. I felt shame; I don't know why I felt responsible, I don't know why.

The doctor suggested that I seek counsel afterward, but I didn't. For the very first time in my life, I felt so painfully alone. I couldn't bring myself to tell Chuck; I don't know why. Perhaps I thought he might have blamed me as well.

I don't know what I felt. But I had six weeks to stay distant because the doctor told me not to have sex till then. That week was the beginning of a series of events that would turn my life upside down.

When I arrived home, there was an eviction notice in the

door! What the hell? Paul was supposed to pay for this. That week my dear uncle passed away, and the following Friday, my father-in-law died as well. That was just the tip of the iceberg as I got the phone call that my brother (or one I call my brother) was murdered. In my efforts to try to keep it together, I began to drink. All in all, I had three deaths, and Paul left me with a bill for $2500.00 in back rent, and I also lost a baby, and his / her father has no clue of its existence all in a 30day period. With all the stress, my performance at work suffered, and I was quickly fired.! My world was quickly coming to an end, and I didn't want to see anyone, especially Chuck. I never got a chance to tell him that my pregnancy was confirmed, let alone that our baby had just died because I wasn't paying attention. I lay in my bed clutching on the card I had for him, the one that set congratulations, you're going to be a daddy again. Crying so hard it hurt, I forced myself to the bathroom and burned it, watching the flames, just like my life, disintegrate. I stand a great chance of being homeless again. I couldn't do this again. I quickly picked up the pieces, and by the end of the week, I was asking around to find who would loan me the money to pay my back rent. After applying at every agency, I had but one person who I hadn't asked. Chuck. But how can I face him? We've passed the 6-week mark, and I have been telling him the great lie that I have been busy or out with the girls. To the girls, I had been hanging with Chuck, and they assumed that's why they haven't seen me accept at the funerals.

I just didn't have the strength. The guilt ate away at me.

So, I did my own memorial I don't know if it was a boy or girl, so I termed it, Angel. I kept a white candle lit daily. It was the only thing that gave me comfort.

The summer came as I was still in debt; I sent the kids to live with their father because I could not feed them. The lights had eventually gotten turned off, as did the cable.

This was my life once again at the entrance of hell…Alone.

It was because I had given the excuse of hanging out all the time that Chuck would not help me. How could I party so much if I am having such financial difficulty? I do not know why I just didn't tell him what position Paul left me in; perhaps it was my fear kicking in. I knew once I opened up, I would tell Chuck about Angel and the shame and the guilt it had left in me.

Chuck called me and called me often, and I could not bring myself to pick up the phone. I couldn't face him. Sitting on my bed listening to his last message." My mother always said when people don't want to be bothered, they will show you," So I'm not going to bother you anymore; I don't know what happened but thank you for being a part of my life. "Take care" dial tone.

At that very moment is when I realized that I loved Chuck so much, for so many valid reasons, I felt like my heart had been ripped right from my chest. I wanted to pick up the phone and just pour out everything, yet my fear was bigger than my desire.

It was this very series of events that led up to me losing Chuck, at least in the manner of that which we shared. Anything else would-be hidden emotion with time spent together, and I would no longer be treated the same. A treatment I accepted as my way of dealing with such a loss. That night in my mind, there was nothing left for me to live for. I pulled out my vodka and drank my woes away. It was the longest night of my life until sleep had its way with me.

It was only ten o'clock in the morning; the sun had already begun to shine on the streets of New York. My head still pounding from my bottle the night before. I headed to the terrace to have my morning cigarette; the memory hit me that by five pm today, I would be losing this apartment. A warm spring breeze flew past me as if to say it's ok, girl, no need to worry. But I have disregarded that message as I stood on the opposite side of the balcony of my twelve-story apartment in Lefrak City, Queens. I looked below with envy as I watched people moving about, most likely on their way to work. Dressed for success, I could even hear some crowds of laughter.

"Must be nice to laugh," I thought to myself. But laughter was no longer a luxury in my life. Wiping the tears from my eyes, I began to feel a bit dizzy, and my belly was filled with nausea. I was so afraid and angry.

"Might as well get this over with," said aloud. I went back into my apartment and straight to the safe in my closet. There was my answer, Paul's 38 caliber, which he forgot to take. I removed all but one bullet. Just do it fast, I thought to myself.

Standing back on my twelve-story terrace, I made sure the safety was off, "I love you, Charles" was all I uttered. I could feel my heart palpitating.

Looking down, I thought maybe I should just jump. But I was a coward, it would take too long, and I wanted to die fast and painless.

I raised the gun to my temple and pulled the trigger.

Nothing happened! "Shit!" I screamed. I placed the gun back to my temple and pulled the trigger again. Still nothing!

Are you serious, God! I walked off the terrace and int5o my bedroom with the gun still in my hand. I placed it on the coffee table and headed back again for the terrace. I no longer cared anymore. I stood there for hours, just crying, and feeling so insignificant and so lost. The memory of my past two marriages flew through my mind confirming that I was never going to be loved. These men always tell you they love you; they don't love me!" They just want me for what lays between my legs! "Isn't that right world? I began to yell aloud. You could give two shits if I jump," I thought to myself (laughing amid my pain).

Yes, that is what I thought. "I hate you, God, you played me! *You* played me! You let them do this to me! You left me just like everyone else, and even you said you loved me!

Yes, you did. I heard you when you said it!" My words trembling like my body, which is by now sweaty and dirty from crying.

Tired and mentally exhausted.

How did I get here, to this place of desperation? Where death seemed to be the only way for me to be free from this current pain. I believed God owed me a different life other than this one.

I would not wait until he decided when I would die; hell, he decided everything else, and it was not working for me.

Damn!

Nothing is going right.

However, I would not let God win. Death would be the one thing that I would have any control over, and I have been singing to the tune of this world and the people in for too long, lying on my back thinking it was love. I kept looking back at my telephone, which had been ringing endlessly; leave me alone! I yelled as if an actual person stood there disturbing me, then my answering machine came on. I heard the voice of my Medea. "Annie Mae, you home? You ok, call me, something doesn't feel right, and I want to make sure you ok' this is mother, are you there"? "Alright, well, call me when you get this message. "Take care" Mother loves you" Mom hangs up. The pain in my heart that appeared while I listened to her voice was overwhelming. "No, mommy, I'm not alright I said aloud" My body wouldn't move to pick up the phone and talk to her; there was just too much going on, and I was in the mood to hear mom preach about God, not today, I just didn't want to hear it. I was empty. My husband, Paul Anderson, the man I surrendered my whole life to decide he wanted a divorce and moved out. All I did was love him, take care of him, and this is what I get for it! He leaves me in financial disarray, and at five pm today, the courts will be taking back their apartment. I will be homeless once again. "All my so-called friends and family have a million reasons why I cannot stay with them. I just had a miscarriage, and that child didn't belong to Paul. I was afraid and ashamed, and God was not helping me. Why? What did I do wrong? I cannot fix it, I don't want to try anymore, and I am tired! "I have nothing left; I have no way out"! My head was consumed with thoughts overflowing with debates on emotions, actions, and emptiness. It was overwhelming.

Is this what it has come down to?

This thought popped in my head out of the blue. Appearing like a movie script, a picture jumped into the mind of my body plastered on the pavement, bloodied, broken wearing my red nightgown, and a loud voice said NO! It's not time for you to go! The question came as quick as lightning right before a storm, "Was my life really so bad that I'm standing here twelve stories high right over the Long Island Expressway all because of a low life bastard of a man that called himself my husband of ten years!

The stronger side of me begins to speak to my senses. Are you actually about to abandon your children as your parents did to you because of fear? "What the hell are you doing?" I said aloud, still standing on the terrace. I began to verbally tell God my feelings.

"My God, why the hell did you even place me here? You are supposed to be kind and loving and deliver me from evil, yet all you have done was place evil in my path! You selected my mother, you selected my father, and this is what they have produced a broken, bitter, and violated woman with a broken soul.

Instead of finishing this vodka, I ought to just saturate myself in it and set myself a flame; after all, you said I am going to hell anyway regardless of if it was my fault or not. The pain could not be any worse. I have bowed down and worshipped, and still, my life is a piece of shit! Chuck made me feel ways no one can put into words and losing my Angel, I felt so disconnected from life and everything in it. I was ready to end it. Let my children's father take care of them. It was at this moment that I have felt so very empty to the point I wanted to die. I had spent, or rather I had given up my power to the point that death seemed like my only option.

"No, not yet" I thought aloud. 'Let me go outside and get some air," I talking to myself. I cleaned myself up, got dressed, then grabbed my keys my purse and headed out the door. 'You need to write this down, I heard in the back of my mind. 'What the hell? I thought, "Sigh" "Alright girl, you think too much, give it a rest" At this point, I was having a girl-to-girl dialogue within myself. Anything, to forget about my pain. I looked around to find a bench where no other occupants would disturb my quiet time.

Didn't want to be bothered. I found one about five feet from a huge oak tree. At least, I think it was an oak tree; it stood tall, full, and bloomed white flowers. I smelled what appeared to be a jasmine fragrance each time the wind blew. Perhaps it wasn't an oak tree; l laughed inside. The sun beaming down on me, I raised my face so that it could caress me with its heat. Secretly hoping God would talk to me but to no avail.

"Hey lady, what you are doing here by yourself?" My peace was distracted by an eerie female voice. It was my neighbor Nicole, who lived three doors down. On a daily basis, I could hear loud arguments from her house that would always end with security coming to her home to shut it down. Naturally, when she sat next to me. She didn't look as bubbly as she sounded, though. I also noticed her hair was out of control, and it was obvious she, too, had been crying.

"You got a light? I got to smoke my mood away. I lit her cigarette for her, as people tend to start talking, and the next thing you know, you have no lighter. Nicole didn't wait for an invite to talk, nor do I think she was concerned if I even wanted to be bothered.

"Zelda, how do you do it? You seem to have it so together, every time I see you, you're like a shining like a ray of light" I laughed, "I don't know what you smoking.

Nicole, but there ain't no rays of light over here" "Trust me, Zelda, I hear people around here, talk about how you're like the fucking Dear Abby of Queens and shit, and you're like some deep chick," I heard you helped Tyra, Patricia, and Tracy and I heard how you got Karen and her man back together. "Please enlighten me, because I can't," Before she could finish her sentence, a waterfall of tears fell, and I couldn't help but embrace her and tell her what advice I could that I felt would help her circumstance. That's just what women do.

It's going to be ok, ladies.

There is always one song that gets people off to the dance floor.

Back then, it was the electric slide. We were doing the slide having a blast, and then Cora motioned me to come with her outside for a smoke.

"Listen, girl, I have a solution to your money problem, but before I tell you, you have to swear not to mention it because no one knows what I do." Already it sounded like prostitution or selling drugs. I had to put it out there, "I don't deal, and my body isn't for sale, but thanks anyway." Cora laughed, "No boo, it's not like that." "Have you ever heard of swapper parties"? "Swapper what? No, what's that"? Feeling extremely slow. Looking around as if to see if anyone was listening. "It's when couples share each other's partner." "Ouch, gross, and unsafe," was my reply. "But no, you don't have to participate you just provide the place to hold it and serve finger foods and shit." "I'm telling you; I have been looking for a job for almost 5 months, and if I wasn't hosting these parties, my ass be in the streets along with my kids because they daddy and just like your baby daddy ready to take them in you feel me?

Hmm, it had my mind thinking.

$340 to pay the electric bill, $170 for my cable, and I'm now at $4250.00 in rent arrears. So, what do I have to do? I asked? Curious and desperate, I gave her my number, and we agreed to talk about it more the next day.

We headed back into the club, and the sound of Destiny's Child was blasting in the air. "I'm a survivor,

I'm not gonna give up; I'm going to work harder." As if they were talking directly to me, I danced toward the floor, and all the images of pain came rushing in my head. I began to cry right there; while I was dancing, it turned into a praise dance, so to speak, people moved out the way, and I didn't realize that as I was singing, crying, and dancing, I had an audience! When the song changed, I was still smiling and

I took a deep breath, "I'm going to make it," I said to my mind, I can do this, I got this. The fact that I had no clue as to how I was going to make it didn't matter, as long as I knew I would make it.

I decided to go and grab another drink before our freebie wore out. I noticed Nicole talking to a few people at the bar. I didn't want to intrude, so I found my own little area and ordered my drink. "What, are you drinking lady, I heard," turning around to see a tall solid bald-headed man dressed very sharp. A black suit, "I'm good, but thank you, I said"

'I'm Greg, he said, and you are? Unavailable was what I said in my mind, but no need to be rude. Jazz, I replied. Would you do me a favor, Jazz, and save a dance for Me.? The bartender brought my drink just in time. I make no promises, I replied as I walked off, drink in hand. I heard a whole lot of damn! Ouch!

That's a fine sister there! etc., but it didn't faze me, I was in a state of heartbreak, and if it wasn't Chuck, I really wasn't interested.

I managed to make it back before the sun came up into my apartment. My dark, loveless, lifeless, foodless apartment.

I realized just how depressed and just how serious my situation was. I have less than 30 days to pay the rent arrears or give up the apartment. Unemployment was nowhere enough but at least on Monday when it arrives, I can put the lights back on and get some groceries, I thought to myself.

I looked around my apartment and surveyed it skillfully. I was seriously considering hosting a swap party. Not forever, but until I find a job.

Yvette and I met over breakfast at Four Brother's restaurant. An establishment well known for home cooking and great customer service that people would drive from miles throughout Queens to enjoy.

As I listened to all the ins and outs of this new venture, I was amazed that people actually did these kinds of things.

Boy, you just never know.

I was filled with questions, and Yvette was able to have a valuable answer for them all.

From here on end, you might want to give yourself a different name, people tend to talk, and you don't want your real you in the mix said Yvette" I thought of the name I gave the guy at the bar and decided my new name would be Jasmine or Jazz for short.

Great, said Yvette; I will help you set the place up on Thursday; you can go with me to a meet tonight to see what actually happens. "Go with you" I don't want to go, I laugh,

I'm not having sex with a bunch of some strangers. We laugh, "You don't have to participate, and there are a lot of people who just watch their called voyeurs. "Ok, this is getting weird. I laughed while inside I cursed Paul for me being in this spot; why tell me you paid the next two months' rent if you didn't. I would

155

have taken the kids out of private school, and I would have had it then. I would have been just grieving instead of grieving and stressing, and I wouldn't have lost my damn job. That fucking bastard, I hope his car falls off a bridge. "Ok, come back, girl, don't go cursing others, you know better than that" my conscious has a way of stepping in when it wants to, not when it needs to.

I wasn't sure what to expect when I went with Yvette to this swap meet, but I made sure that I was not dressed sexy, just casual. I didn't want anyone looking at me in that fashion, and I was not seeking to even converse with them. Yvette and I met at the Dunkin Doughnuts on 57th avenue.

The popular hangout spots. "You look awfully casual she stated." 'It's on purpose I chuckled. You're a scary cat girl, you will be fine, relax, if anyone comes toward you and you're not interested, just say no thanks. That's how it's done. There is security there, so if you can't find me go to security if somebody becomes a pest or annoying. It took all but a fifteen-minute ride before we got there. A very tall apartment building overlooking Queens Botanical Garden. It definitely was not the project, more like a condominium.

As soon as we got out of the cab, Yvette's popularity was evident. 'Hey, girl! A woman waved as she and a few others headed toward the lobby. "There were two elevators, and I was glad we entered the elevator with the least people. I already felt cheap, and we weren't even at the event yet. The door opens, and there is a table a few feet away that you had to stop by and sign in. Sign in? I don't want to put my name down on anything, then I remember that tonight I am not Zelda; I am Jazz. I also observed that the men paid, not the women. "How you doing, girl, you ok" asked Yvette, ensuring I would be ok.

I'm good, I replied, yet inside shaking like a leaf. We entered the apartment at the end of the hall. The lighting was soft, and there was a room that said Ladies knock first. Yvette knocked, and a heavy-set woman opened the door to let us in. This is Trish said Yvette; she secures the ladies' dressing room, so you don't have to worry about your personals being taken.

Trish gives me a smile, "Hey, newbie, enjoy yourself, play safe, and the word for the night is Peaches" Peaches? What does that mean? I asked, feeling like a first grader on a college playground. It means 'No". That's all you need to say if someone approaches, and you're not interested.

Wow, I laughed, well call me Del Monte because I'm going to peach everyone I see tonight. We all laughed.

Yvette began to take off her clothes, you don't have to participate, but you can't enter fully dressed. You're good since you're wearing that camisole &thongs. Get the hell out of here, you serious? Nice for you to tell me that ahead of time. I didn't feel too bad with what I had on, it's basically a nighty, and it's not see-through.

We walked around, and my eyes couldn't believe half the things it was seeing! It's like being on the set of a porn movie. Inside I felt so much shame, on the outside, all I could think of was whatever it took to get my kids back and secure a roof over my head. I positioned myself in a corner with a few other women who were just there to watch. Voyeurism. I lit my cigarette and observed my surroundings.

Red lights, which gave the room an erotic atmosphere; there were several oil burners carefully placed around every table, sending the fragrance of musk and opium into the air. And on every table lie various condoms for men and women of different sizes and flavors. The instrumental music playing was quite sensuous. A mix of Janet Jackson lyrics mixed in it gave off a pretty cool and relaxing vibe, and no one had approached me yet, so I was at ease.

With all the oohs and ahs in the air, my eyes locked on a couple on the right standing on the wall. The woman had her arms up and her back to the wall, just a small pouch that said she had a child or children, her legs firm, and a mocha tone complexion. Her makeup was flawless, and although her breast wasn't as full, her overall appearance was actually beautiful, her companion was a male, built like he worked out on a regular basis. He was pouring oil on her slowly and massaged it from her arms and worked his way down. I have to be honest to say it was turning me on; in the back of my mind, I pictured him being Chuck and her being me. All the moments I never got to have with him, after being there for about an hour, my consciousness kicked in, and I had to remove myself. I was becoming tempted and that's when I knew it was time to leave. I didn't take any time trying to find Yvette, I simply went and got dressed and called a cab and left. When I got home, I held my pillow and played that scene over and over in my mind. With Floetry playing on my cd, "say yes," I mustered up the nerve to dial Chuck's number, even after all this time has passed, I know it very well. I just called to hear his voice, when he said hello, I hung up. Still can't face him, too much shame. I took this moment to think on what my next move should be. I had already applied to various Government and Charitable agencies to get rent assistance, and I was denied since I couldn't show how I will be able to continue paying rent on my own. I sent my resume to as many job openings I could think of, and well, now I'm in the hands of fate, and fate apparently isn't paying attention to my moment of urgency.

I set it in stone, and I would host my first swap party at

the end of the week. I used some of my unemployment to set up everything similar to what I had seen at the party the other night. Yvette was my word of mouth.

I would need to move quickly, and Yvette knew I would need twenty people to pay $30 a night for the next 5 nights so that I would least be able to give the court something and get an extension. 'Girl don't play with the court; you need $4000.00 let's make that the goal. I got you.' She was good. I don't know who or how, but the very first night was crazy. I had a packed house. I had to pull myself up mentally all day; I was really dreading to have to step this low, but until I can find a job, I need to be able to support my children, and in doing that, I need this rent money so shame would have to take a back seat to my reality.

I comforted myself by remembering that as long as I don't sleep with anyone, I'm not giving up my morals or cheating on

Chuck, even though we weren't together.

I dressed as a host would, off-limits but eye candy, wearing a one-piece satin lingerie gown, split on the side, and black toe-out heels! I was standing out for sure. My gown was see-through, and my thongs were visible. The only thing different about my party was I interacted with the guest, making sure they were all satisfied. I talked to them, I built a rapport with them,

160

and I served their drinks. At one point, everyone stopped having sex, and they were listening as I was giving advice to one couple, and soon enough everyone join in.

Most of my guests were people in high positions or careers that required silence to be a golden rule. I was more than happy to oblige.

One of my guests asked the question I hoped would never come up" you were at the last Party, but you never partake; what's up with that? In my efforts to hide my shame, I flipped it and responded with humor, "looksee's no feels. They all laughed. But seriously, I do this as a temporary Brenda for an immediate situation, I have a few things I need to take care of like asap, that's the only reason I'm doing it. No pun intended, though.

What is it you need to do? No need to be personal, if we can trust you to be silent, you should be able to trust us. Nervously, I began to open up to my new group of elite friends. In a nutshell, I married a bastard that left me in rent arrears, and I had to send the kids away; that was it, the tears fell, and the story came out. There was so much hugging going on, I was shocked. These were not bad people, just people who lived out what they want without hurting anyone else.

When I said how much I needed, one of my guests replied, "hell, if we all come back with a guest, we can get that resolved." Long story short, by the end of the week, I had earned $6000.00! Grateful enough to buy me an extra two months to find a job and keep the rent paid. As it turns out, the very crowd that I was so quick to judge had made them available to me to prevent me from being homeless. Once again.

I managed to find a job a few months later through a reference from one of my guests that were in real estate, but not before I hosted at least five more parties. When I look back, I have to laugh. There is a secret world where the elite go. The big dogs and the money makers that we look up to that help us, and some of them are our very own leaders, and here they are, swapping girlfriends, wives, and husbands. The irony is you never know who's doing what with whom when out of the limelight.

My group of friends changed as a result of this lifestyle. I would get calls from some of them giving them advice etc. I never got paid for it, and I never thought to ask for compensation. I eventually became the relationship and sex Guru, so to speak. I read every book I could get my hands on about phycology, relationships, sex, and, of course, stayed in my bible. I continued attending the swap parties and took mental notes. Planning in my mind to write a book or at least be able to share what I learned with the friends that asked me about sex ideas and advice. Who knew what I was lining up for as I look back at it now?

Back Together Again

Christmas was coming close, and I was missing Chuck more and more. Wondering if he had the same phone number, I decided I would be bold and text him instead of calling him, just in case he's angry with me, I won't feel so humiliated. "Happy Holidays' was all I texted. Nothing more. Twenty minutes later, he responded with "same to you!" I was so excited! Just to have the lines of communication open was enough for me. Fate was generous to me, and Chuck and we had started seeing each other once again, yet, after a while, it was not the same, but

I was grateful, nonetheless. I couldn't expect him to be the same after I left him. So, I embraced moments shared, and it was enough to sustain me.

But we would not have New Years that year; this told me that I would now be treated with as much care as he delivered in the beginning. I accept that; I deserved that. In my mind, I still had hopes that we could rekindle, and I could regain my status with him.

Although I had a job, the money earned was barely enough for anything extra. I was still struggling. Paul still came around to pick up our son and kept him on the weekends and some holidays. One of my new elite friends planted a seed in my head I never thought of. "Why aren't you getting child support from him? You know what, with all that was going on, that never even crossed my mind. With all the family deaths and the miscarriage, I was overwhelmed, and basic strategies never crossed my mind. I went down to the courts first thing in the morning to get the ball rolling. $800.00 a month! That's what I would receive for one child, exhaling in tears; I wanted to slap myself for not thinking about this sooner. Even greater was I would receive back pay for the whole year from the date he moved out. Oh, I love the system.

You want to watch a man squirm go for his pockets. In a matter of three weeks of being served, all of a sudden, Paul was calling me to tell me how he was still in love with me and wanted his family back. Are you kidding me! Those days are over. The only one I have had sex with was Chuck, and I was definitely satisfied, and while Chuck has still not made us official, I would hold on with him. I still have the challenge of getting into his mind and having him open up more. I want to know him; I need to know him. His dreams and desires, his goals, his beliefs, how he grew up, etc.

But due to my foolishness, I may never have that opportunity. Yet, my heart would never let it go, it would always beat with hope.

The company I worked for lost the contract it had, which meant once again I was unemployed. Dam, here we go again! My kids are here, so I will defiantly not be hosting any more parties.

My combined income with child support and unemployment with be a monthly $1400.00. My rent was $1250.00. I did have a few hundred dollars put to the side, and my credit card still had $500.00 availability. I would be ok for a few months, I think. I didn't want to ride on this merry-go-round with Paul or Chuck, for that matter. I had to know where I stood with Chuck. I called him, and during our conversation, Angel kept coming to mind, but I would not put that burden upon him. It would be unfair. I did, however, ask him the following. "Do you see us as a couple in the near future?" "I can't answer that Chuck stated" "Why not?" it's a very simple question, do you feel like I am the one that you want to build with, and it's just you and me? Or do you see yourself coming and going dating but not serious. So basically, what I am asking is, do you see me in your future? "I won't be upset; I just need to know."

'No, said Chuck, I don't see that"

I was crushed, but I couldn't let it show. "Ok, that wasn't so bad now, was it"? Trying not to show that I was fighting tears and clenching my fist and feeling like a fool. "I'll talk to you later, sweetie, have a good one." His reply made the dial tone seem extremely loud and painful. I tossed my phone at my mirror, unconcerned over the shit of seven years' bad luck. Hell, I've been living more than seven years of bad luck; life owes me a few refunds. That's it; I'm pretty much done with love. Sure, some of you would probably say there's plenty of fish in the sea, the problem with that was I didn't want to go into the sea anymore, I don't even want to get wet for that matter. If real love did not want anyone else, then I was in it. I've tried my best to get Chuck back, and it's not going to happen. Paul, all of a sudden, has this love that I know is called I don't want to pay you child support. Time to tune into my inner bitch.

In the words of Delores Claiborne, "sometimes being a bitch is all a woman has."

So, Paul, you want to play with my life and shit with my feelings. I got something for you. You won't pay $800.00 a month, but you will get these children and me out of the city and into a house in the south. We both understood the reason we were getting back together. Meanwhile, everyone decided I was so wrong for doing this, forgetting the fact that Paul's infidelity got me in this single status in the first place.

So off to the big ATL we went, in our new home, or should I say house; I went into this for the wellbeing of my children. This man did not want me, it was clear, and it was spoken. I would use this time to focus on connecting to God and furthering my education without having to worry about being separated from my children. It was a mere year before Paul found another floozy to have an affair with and in my house. Every neighborhood has that one nosey person that sees who comes and goes, and they are always willing to let you know. Well, as it seems that while I was practicing my ministry, giving bible study classes on Wednesday, Paul had a woman in my house. She had never been married and was a bit older than me. I always question a woman that old who has never been married. In any event, before I jumped to conclusions, I would check the condom count. (Yes, I made him wear them when we did have sex, for various reasons, but mostly because since Angel left my body; I didn't feel right having anyone

167

other than Chuck inside me. Perhaps my way of never forgetting. Plus, who knows what Paul has been up to. In any event, there were ten (we had only lain together twice that month). With that in mind, I left to give my class, but not before Paul asked if I was taking the kids with me. Red light! When your man/woman starts asking questions on the obvious, it is being done for confirmation. Never forget this point! "I always take them with me," eyebrow up and not surprised at all.

That night when I came back, there were nine condoms, and Paul was sitting down at his computer. What made it worse was that her purse was there sitting on my coffee table!

The mark of a true bitch! You couldn't just leave us the hell alone; you don't have one of your own, so into my cave, you dabbled.

There is nothing worse than the Jezebel that enters into the cave of a lioness! That is the lowest level a female can stoop to. It didn't matter that there were bloodstains on my mattress and that my bathroom smelled of Raspberry soap. The soap I never use! I had nothing left inside, numb, and I could give a dam on anything he did from that moment on. My priorities were my children's wellbeing. I would no longer worry about who loved me or wanted me.

I registered for school and worked toward every

certification I could think of to keep busy and build a nest of my own. I continued going to church and accepted my calling to ministry. It was no longer a concern of relationships but of God. How can I get God to see me? How can I make my prayers heard?

It was easy as pie, being able to help other people. I didn't have to go searching for them; they simply appeared as if God had guided them to me. I found my joy watching the results that some would call me and tell me their marriage is better after my counsel, or that someone who had self-esteem issues is now empowered or even more so to know that I helped someone escape from domestic abuse. I have come across a lot of these types of people, and truth be told, they give me strength. I would not allow myself to be dependent on a man. I worked at the daycare full time and took classes online. I was not giving up. Going into year two was when it hit me that I hadn't had sex; it was my birthday, and naturally, the first person I thought of was Chuck. Darn! Why can't I get this man off my brain, in all the years

I have known him; he's still there. We made love like we never parted whenever we had the chance. As fate would have it, he just so happened to be in my area of the south, and of course, we met up. Still handsome as ever, still has the potential to make me forget my common sense and open myself to foolish possibilities.

I will never understand it when people say God is teaching us something when bad things happen. For all I have been through, I don't need any lessons; I need blessings. Two months after I saw Chuck, I became pregnant…again. This time I had been told that my body would not be able to carry it; my body apparently suffered from progesterone insufficiency and a uterine abnormality.

Which simply meant my uterus is tilted to some degree. My doctor asked me if I wanted to set an appointment for my left tube to be re-connected. No, let it be. Little did I know that later in life, fibroids would come into play as well, and I would have to suffer losing one more child. I don't remember what sparked a really big argument with Chuck and me on the phone on a summer afternoon. Something to the sound of me telling him, "Damn you!" And his reply was yes; damme for messing with a married woman!" That statement cut me deeper than anything that happened to me throughout the course of my life. Did he not hear me, did he not believe me, that ever since I have known him, he has become my husband in my heart? Did he not understand that no man would enter my gates while he was in my life? That no other man mattered? Chuck never understood even to the day that he was my air. There was a safety felt in his presence that I didn't' understand. But it gave me a sense of security. I would play it over and over on my mp3 player,

"NO AIR," Jordon Sparks, my heart's only way to explain how it felt.

All kinds of thoughts ran through my head, like how the pain life can bring to us and the choices we make to survive will forever follow us. I thought about times we will lose those we love, be judged by those who say they care and talked about in the worst way by those who don't understand.

We have the power that if only we stay plugged in to "our inner God," we can change every outcome to the desired manifestation we so choose. In order to even reach this plateau, we must first grab hold of our emotions and put them in the proper place. We make decisions based on how we are feeling about the current situation. This is a dangerous way to live. Most of the time.

When situations arise, no matter how they occur, no matter who is responsible for them, we must learn to reply, not react. Think of what we would like the outcome to be (which requires mastering our thinking skills), then reply to our answers suitable for the current moment.

Another Chance at Love

    This new era of the internet worked out for me in ways I would have never thought of. Have you ever had those moments where you haven't given thought to someone in such a long time?

    Then unexpectedly, their name comes to mind. I hadn't given Darren Witherspoon too much thought since his sister told me he had gotten married and was in the military. I was so tired of Paul's games, even now that we're in Georgia; I'm still seeing the old man who found yet and still the need to shit around on me. No sex in two years because he wouldn't touch me. Yeah, I'm doing me by going to school and such, but hell, a girl still has needs. I spent a lot of my time in my home office listening to Mary J Blige and every sad song of feeling unloved that was on the charts. Feeling lower than I have ever felt in my life (and I have had some low points), but this moment was different; I was famished for love. Yet it was nowhere around me. Even the small moments with Chuck couldn't sustain me anymore. I wanted more. Therefore, I went playing around on the famous social media platform they called Myspace. It was fun; I created a profile and posted my best picture. Now what? Ok, let's friend some of our old friends.

The first person I thought of (and I don't know why) was Louvain Hayes. Typing in the last name and eager to see if she faces. Nevertheless, she wasn't on Myspace. Low and behold, the very first picture that came up with that last name was Darren Witherspoon! Wow! What an omen, you think? I hesitated and just stood looking at his picture on the screen. What do I say? What can be said to someone you simply stopped seeing? I had just never gone back.

All the memories came flashing through my mind. Frightened at what the result would be. Would he be angry? Would he remember me? Would he even respond?

Boldly I sent him a message that went like this:

Hi, is this Darren Witherspoon, Brenda's brother? This is

Zelda; would you ask her to stop by my page. Take care. I didn't want to be insulted or humiliated, so I refrained from discussing us. It took a whole 30 days, and still no response. I guess he's still upset after all these years. I can't blame him. I left to head home and never returned. Low and behold, thirty-three days later, there it was! In my inbox, a letter from Darren Witherspoon.

Short and sweet. "Yes, this is Darren Witherspoon, Brenda's brother. You and I have a lot to talk about, I'm sure. Call me, 850-555-3333". Wow! Ok, slow down, girl.

What do I do know, I asked myself?

I picked up my phone and nervously called him. He answered a firm hello. Hi, it's I, Zelda. That was all I could muster. As it turned out, we talked for over three hours before Darren Witherspoon stated he wanted to see me and would be coming down to GA in three days to see me.

I was so nervous. But I was lonelier than nervous, so we met at a hotel, three exits away. Ironically, Chuck called me the same day to tell me he was in town at the same hotel, room 102! I had to make a choice between being with the man who had my heart but wouldn't make me his or the man who I knew years ago who was seeking the same thing I was seeking. A family. I took a moment to weigh my options, and I decided that if I were going to have a life of being loved and having a family, then Darren

Witherspoon would be the door I must knock-on. Even if it doesn't work out, at least I know I'm heading into a relationship where we at least want the same things. Room 212. I knocked on the door, my heart racing like a NASCAR driver right before a big race. He didn't change a bit. Just older, that curve in his chest was still there. I was everything except disappointed. We talked for hours about everything from relationships to religion. I felt alive again. I agreed to take a trip from GA to Pensacola, FL, to visit him the following week. This I would do since Paul decided he was going to take a trip to New York with the kids. I knew he was at his ex-wife's house since children don't know about silence.

When Paul called me to let me know, they arrived at his "mothers' home, I ask to speak to our son. Hi, mommy said my little one with such excitement in his tone. Are you having fun with daddy? I asked. Oh yeah, we at Ms. Cora's house' we are spending the night." It took everything in my mouth to contain my disapproval. Ok, I said, well, you have fun and be a good boy, ok." I could hear the crickets in the background; apparently, they didn't warn him not to tell me where he was. Tell daddy mommy said "goodbye_" ok said Travis Jr, and like any child, he dropped the phone, and I heard him playing around, and of course, someone hung up the phone. Which was fine; there was nothing left to say. It's officially over.

While I am not one for driving, let alone a six-hour trip by myself. I felt in my heart it was high time to do something different. The drive was scary as it began to rain cats and dogs as soon as I hit I-65. Shall I turn around or keep moving. For once in my life, I am going to move forward despite the storm in front of me. I was scared as hell, but I kept pushing. I would meet my prince charming and enjoy this three-week vacation.

By the second week, Darren Witherspoon had given me a key to the house, and looking me in my eyes, he told me, "we're going to finish what we started.'

The next month, we went and picked out a beautiful blue diamond ring that he put on my finger and asked me to marry him. Trying to make this a decision that would not hurt me, I told him, I will marry you, but I will not make any moves until God tells me to move. Fair enough, he said. In my mind, I knew there was still much I needed to know about Darren Witherspoon. It had been twenty-four years. I didn't want any more surprises in my life.

The summer was coming to an end. I had been enjoying this time on the beach with Darren Witherspoon; in my heart, Chuck still lived, but I knew we would never be. I deserved to be happy; I deserved to be with someone who loved and appreciated me and all that I brought to the table. I deserved a life. So, I headed back to that place Paul called home. Strategically, I had everything I was going to take already packed and in the garage. As soon as Paul walked into the house with the kids, he did something he hadn't done in two years. He kissed me and said, "we need to talk" Laughter burst in my brain, and I did my best to keep the silence. I simply gave him "the look" and proceeded to welcome the children home. That night as I continued with my normal procedure, as far as I was concerned, nothing had changed. I had been sleeping with a blanket, and a pillow on the floor in our bedroom, and Paul never cared then; however, now, suddenly, he wants me to come to bed. Pretty soon, this laughter is going to fall out of my mouth. "I'm leaving you, Paul." There, I said it. Leaving me? As if he was surprised. Why? I laughed aloud. I couldn't hold it in anymore. 'Why?

Are you kidding me? You haven't touched me in two years, you're having an affair with your daughter's mother, your ex-wife, and you're asking me why? Paul's face switched to a child who just was caught with his hand in the cookie jar.

"Baby, please come get in the bed; we can work this out.

I'm sorry" Get in bed! You've watched me sleep on the floor, stepped over me, and ignored me as if I was a piece of shit, now you want me to get in the bed"? No, thanks, Paul, I'm fine right where I am. Paul suddenly found tears to muster, which meant absolutely nothing to me at this point.

Do you know how many times I have cried? How many endless nights do I spend pacing back and forth over our marriage?

How many times I have tried to hold you, only for you to push me away and tell me," It's not you, it's me? You can cry until Jesus comes back, honey, and it wouldn't mean a thing to me. You can't have your cake and eat it too. You've trampled my heart one too many times; now it belongs to someone else. "Paul lifts his head and has the nerve to ask me," so what are we going to do" We? I asked. 'We aren't going to do anything, I replied. I'm looking for a place as we speak, and I'm moving out and taking the kids with me. Then I laid my head down on my so-called bed on the floor and closed my eyes in my attempt to sleep. It took me a while to drift off, for, in my heart, it felt as if a heavyweight had just been lifted.

Suddenly I could breathe! Suddenly I felt alive! Suddenly I felt no longer bound but free. Moreover, not because of another man, but because I finally pushed myself to take a stand and free myself. It was the most exhilarating feeling I have ever encountered. The next morning Paul behaved as if last night never happened. However, oh no, I would not let you rob me of my independence. So, when he left the house to go to the dentist.

(Unaware that I knew he was with "her again) I packed the kids up and placed a letter reiterating what I had already told him and moved my family to Florida to begin a new journey of peace.

When I arrived in Florida, I wasn't sure what to expect. My greatest concern was if my two children, Jason, and Amber, would be alright emotionally. Sure, I was unhappy, but still, I had to put them first. Darren had asked me to marry him, and although it wouldn't be right away. I said yes. (I still had to deprogram Chuck out of my heart as well as my spirit) This move would give the kids and me a fresh start. They will still get to see their father and yet be in a less stressful home environment with a less stressed mom. They loved it from day one. We went straight to the beach, and I introduced them to Darren. Like all kids, they were still a bit leery, but in time, we all got along as a family. Darren and I got married a year later, yet being married twice before, I didn't want to do the whole big wedding thing. A simple trip to the courthouse with everyone dressed and color-coordinated with a white limo was sufficient. And for a while, we were the perfect family. Or at least that is what I thought. I was so gung-ho about being loved that it didn't dawn on me that I had separated myself from my children emotionally.

This is something we, as women, do.

It's what Philosopher Eckhart Tolle called connecting to the pain body. That moment we connect ourselves to past pain and our actions are based on it, we tend to feed it with an initial moment of satisfaction. In other words, when women find that missing link of the love they've been searching for, they feed it and forget everything and everyone else. This is my sin, and I lived with it for two years before I realized that my children were in pain. What opened my eyes? To start with, my daughter became cold and distant from me, unlike the warm bond we once had. My youngest son turned to weed and such to heal his pain, and even then, I still missed their cries for attention. They were also seeking and had been saturated with the same pain of feeling unwanted. I had passed this curse down to my children. I entered this relationship on my terms, not for the sake of survival but for the need to be loved. I had demonstrated my strength to myself the moment I packed my kids in the car and made a conscious choice to have better and be better. It was at that moment; I created my own song. A song of freedom, love, peace, and happiness. But love was still missing. I felt it with Darren, somewhat, but somewhere in the pit of my soul, there was still an emptiness that screamed loudly. However, I ignored it since I had already made a major move, and fear kept me from investigating further. I simply enjoyed the presence and took no thought of my future. Big mistake.

Women, including myself, are so busy investigating the past lovers in our man's lives to get a glimpse of who we were dealing with. I have discovered that it's his childhood we should be looking into. What a child grows up with plays a massive part in who he will be with his women.

So, what was my goal? What am I attempting in sharing my story and exposing my life to you?

The goal is to spread the message that we, as women, no matter what age, culture, or sexual orientation, hold a profound dark secret truth of "why" we lay our heads on satin pillows and perfumed sheets right beside the very force that inhales our power. It is on that pillow beside that force that we hold our secrets of rape, domestic violence, and more, and these events made us vulnerable every time someone said they loved us. We yearn to be free from that painful body that lives through us, causing us to make poor choices in our partners, time after time. Yet we are still empty. We write songs about it. Finding love, unaware that the moment you realize that you are not getting the "love" that will make you feel free, it is simply time to move forward. Alone. Or, if nothing more, prepare yourself to move forward. This is my crossroad and my moment of taking back my power. This is my life, and I am not your Jezebel. Every so often, I peek behind me and wonder so many what-ifs. But I know I would not be the woman I am today if I didn't step out in faith with every breath of my being. I realized I owed it to myself to be better, have more, and be successful.

To experience life while I still had breathed in my body. Over the years, I have contacted several friends and family members. My father has died during the Covid pandemic from cancer; as for my birth mother, we are still restoring our relationship. At least, to the best of our human forgiveness. As for the mother who raised me, the one I hold in my heart, she has gone on to glory as well. But one month before God called her home; she gave me what I believe was God's answer to the why me question. However, it did not hit me until that painful moment that I watched them close her casket. It took everything in my soul to hold it together, and it felt like my heart was about to burst through my chest from the pain of grief. Yes, I was all grown up and with my own family. Married to Darren, I was now Mrs. Zelda Witherspoon, yet and still at this moment, I felt very much alone.

The memory came as I took my mind back one month before my mother endured that life taking stroke. My adopted mom, adopted brother, and I was sitting at the kitchen table during one of my visits to New York, updating her of my work in life coaching in hopes that it may empower other women in pain. "You know darling, for all that you've been through, your about to be as big as Oprah," I laughed.

"No, really, I mean it, you're going to go places," My brother from another mother laughed and replied, really, mom, where is she going. We all laughed, but I could not help wondering how far this book could go. Just how helpful it would be to others. "Your saving lives, that's all God wanted from you, to "be there" for others like he sent others to you.

The lightning shot off in my mind; my memory took me back to that balcony ledge when I heard the words "write it down." I had not been obedient; I didn't want the world to read my pain and judge me. But her words planted the seed of determination. I began to put to work my life journey down on paper.

Writing, re-writing, being judged, and losing friends, and going back to every journal to get the trials and tribulation correct. I went back to school and began my studies in Psychology; I researched and obtained my certification for life coaching, Domestic Violence Branding, and Intercultural Communication to be official.

I began educating myself with books by great minds like

Aristotle, Socrates, Napoleon Hill, and Ernest Holmes. I took every opportunity to engage in life coaching and public speaking seminars. My most significant moment was the seminar I went to with Les Brown. I learned so much, and little did I know that seminar would change my whole perspective on life. I understood that our life story is the primary tool to empowerment and motiving others. As wild and crazy as it is, my story is not one that cannot be connected with.

We all seek love, unaware that it can never be found in another human being until we discover it within ourselves.

I also began to understand that I was still whole, no matter how much pain I endured. I am still God's Masterpiece, even though when it came to my oppressors, the ones who used me, hurt me, and tried to break me, "they never said sorry."

Process to Restoration

My external freedom did not begin until a year after I moved to Florida and have decided to put the past me. Please start with the following steps of initiation by healing thyself. For only through healing can you see your true self? When you see your true self and accept it, the world will also. Otherwise, if you don't know who you are, the world will tell you, you will believe it, and lack of self is a great sin.

Walk a Black Queens walk, talk a Black Queens talk, and be a Black Queen in the Now. Giving no thought to yesterday.

A Queen does not need to dress in excessive provocativeness, she knows the value of herself. She understands that her body is sacred, and not everyone is entitled to grab a sneak peek at the jewels she beholds. She displays enough to show her beauty, yet not too much to degrade her legacy. Perfect detail is given when she applies her makeup, it shows her power, her magic, her spiritual self. It's magnetic and alluring all at the same time.

When a QUEEN gets dressed for the day, she is sending a

message to the eyes of the world who look upon her. Thus, ask yourself, "What message would I like to send the world today.

A Queen's walk is shoulders back and head high. She is a warrior; she has overcome a lot of shit in her life. Thus, she is confident and demonstrates self-respect. She is aware of her surroundings, never missing an enemy coming or leaving. She sees and hears the snares around her and acts accordingly. She is boss, and she is unapologetic about it. She doesn't follow trends. She creates them, no matter what type of neighborhood she resides in. She is self-educated, reading books that give her real empowerment, spiritual growth, and financial intelligence. She knows when to spend and when to save. A QUEEN is selective in her outgoing information, never giving too much of herself, but just enough to start a chatter. While she is not judgmental, she doesn't apologize for being selective in the company she keeps. She is not arrogant, but she is no weakling either. She makes time for self-care and healing. She doesn't regret her mistakes. Instead, she marks the lessons, careful not to relive them again. A QUEEN is an Alpha but careful not to intentionally offend, however, she will not dumb herself down for anyone.

She is power aware. Whether in an LGBT life or not, a QUEEN is limitless and seeks not revenge, but escalation despite. Every QUEEN must perform a self-initiation to bring to life her new self while being her true self. It is not pretty, but it is necessary.

My first step was "*Acceptance*"

Now what? I asked myself. I am still in pain.

"Forgiveness" Forgiveness would be my second step. Not to those who offended me, but to myself, for the guilt and shame, I allowed myself to feel.

Accountability was the most challenging part in the restoration process because, at first, I did not see how any of this shit that happened to me could be my fault.

After moving my ego out of the way, I remember that I did not have to be homeless; I could have gone back to

Medea's instead of feeling shame simply because I wasn't a virgin. I had forgotten back then that God forgives. I also could have gone back to her instead of fixing a marriage filled with adultery and mental and physical abuse. She was sent to me, and I was so busy trying to remedy situations that I was not supposed to be in, in the first place.

After that awakening thought, I knew I had to make a conscious decision to "let go" that was easy to do since I had accepted and forgiven myself. What also helped me let go was talking about it. Not for sympathy, but for the empowering of someone else who was in the shoes I had once worn. It reminded me that I was ok, that I not only survived, but I overcame, and thus there was no need to hold on to the pain, just the knowledge of the lesson. I took some time to ask myself what exactly it was I wanted in my life. I felt better about the whole tragic life thing, but

I wasn't successful, and I sure didn't feel like Oprah, sure I was helping others, saving lives' empowering my sisters and now my brothers, and even reconnecting marriages. But my pockets were not even big enough to go to the Oprah show, let alone live like her. That is when I had to take some time off from my little social media world and focus on reading and educating myself on wealth building. To know me, to empower myself philosophically and financially. Then I can be an asset to others. But even before all that, I like you with that hope that one last attempt of external love (from another) would begin with me putting my demands on the table. Come what may. Either love me the way I need to be loved and seek your wisdom or let me be, for I have come too far in my life to live the past and re-create the pain all over again. I have learned to love me first, put me first, and this dear reader is what you must grasp. You must come first! I want to prepare your mindset so that you can come to grips with your truth just like me.

Then you will understand how to "apply" the lessons that

will be laid out before you.

As you read, six elements almost made me take my life: rape, domestic violence, abandonment, homeless, and heartbreak. I could blame those elements for my poor choices; however, when you want true freedom, you must go to the source. I was my source. I had the power to choose what I would allow others to do to me, and I did not put that power in place. Those things I had no control over, I still had the ability not to let it keep me hostage, mentally. For years I didn't know that.

Why do you ask?

The truth of the matter is this, folks. There will be elements that we can't avoid. But the moment we decide to allow it to control our lives is when we become victims. The term Jezebel is indeed a biblical term based on a woman who allegedly used her womanly wiles to get what she wanted.

The part of the story that's been left out is how she got that way. For decades, women have been forced to lay on their backs for survival, and it is usually a man playing a significant role in that scene. This is not to male bash; this is just a fact. Think of the position's women have been put into for years. Single mothers abused women, etc. The list is endless, yet we must make a conscious decision to take out power back at some point. I have created a workbook to connect with this book to help you do just that. (The Power of a Woman) The moment you understand that you are not your life circumstance is when you will be able to make better choices. Take a step to become free from the elements that have taunted you since childhood. What is your unspoken experience? And in conclusion, understand that though my story is true, harsh, steamy, and unorthodox, I Ishtar (Goddess), I AM GREATNESS CREATED FROM THE PAIN I CONQUERED!

WORKBOOK

I will ask you a series of questions meant to open your pain door. Don't get angry; get healed. Are you ready? Let's heal. And pull up the "I am not your jezebel playlist. This playlist was selected especially for you, the reader; as you heal, we want to put God in your presence. As reflect on what type of "emotions have been stirred up by all the answers you have just listed. You may be feeling angry or really hurt. But answer anyway. It's for your emotional release and wellbeing.

Have you ever been molested?

If so, at what age?

Have you ever been raped?

If so, at what age?

Have you ever encountered domestic violence? Are you still in a Domestic violent relationship? If you answered yes, ask yourself, why are you still in it? Be honest.

STOP

Write down the relationship you have with your mother

STOP.

Write down the relationship you have with your father.

STOP.

How do you see yourself at this moment as a woman?

STOP.

What challenges are you facing in your personal development?

STOP.

What would you change at this moment about yourself?

You may be feeling angry or hurt, and that's ok.

We want the truth only because it is the truth that sets us free.

Those feelings in you, pain, shame, and anger, have no power over you. You have the power to release it; you don't have to hurt my sister; I have been where you are right now, and when

I pulled that trigger, it wasn't just because of the eviction, it was because I felt like you may be feeling after you write your truth. I felt dirty, angry, used, humiliated, and stressed. But my sister, God has such a plan for you; your storm is over. We both know you wouldn't have made it with the creator. Take this moment and give gratitude. Take this moment and love on yourself.

God saw the best in you when everyone else could see the worst in you. They don't understand your struggle; they don't understand your pain. But oh, to the wonders of the highest, despite your pain, the act is over, you're still here, you have a purpose! You cannot leave this place until your appointed time and your time is not at hand. Put your arms

around yourself and love you. It doesn't matter what you did. You are not a phenomenal woman of God, and nothing nor can anyone take that from you. Do you understand that? Take five minutes and "let these feelings do what they will.

Look in the mirror and tell yourself," I am not a victim! Shout it aloud; I am not a victim!

I am a---------, *AND YOU FILL IN THE BLANK!*

conquer" The enemy have encamped around you since birth, they've been telling you, you're not worthy of love, you're not worthy of success.

Even family wrote you off and said you'd never amount to

anything. But God, God saw the best in you. There is so much more you must do. Head high, eyes open, shameless, that is how a woman of God walks.

LETTING GO THE RIGHT WAY

When we are letting go, it is essential to ensure that we don't take too long in doing it; otherwise, what we end up doing is empowering it. You have come way too far for that, haven't you? So, you have let it out. Thus, it's been accepted by your mind that it has happened. Now what? Blow it to the wind. How? If you remember what the feeling was when you thought of the incident, anytime the feeling returns, you have a responsibility to change your thoughts ASAP. Don't give it excuses that it doesn't work; it will work if you work it. We can ask God all we want, but my dear, there are just times that God will not assist you because he already gave you the power to do it yourself. I learned that the hard way, so how can you change the emotions? Funny how the simplest things are the ones we don't believe will work. It was you and only you that put that image or thought in your mind that caused those feelings, so it is your responsibility to change it. By the way, before you say you didn't know about it, you happened to be around a family member or event, and seeing the enemy brought the memory to you, then sister you owe it to yourself to stay away from those events or people until being around them no longer causes you pain. You got no excuse. Who or what causes you to remember the pain? Knowing this reminds you what to stay away from.

SPIRITUAL THERAPY

We live in a world where everyone seems to be seeking power. But what is power really? What purpose does it serve and how can it give us a feeling of grandeur in this physical world? Webster's dictionary describes Power as: "The ability to influence people, places, and things in one's own environment. "As true as this definition may be, the rabbit hole is much deeper than we realize. I invite you to swallow the red pill and open your mind to an understanding of not man's mere definition of power, but of a power larger than life, it is Inner God power, and we don't have to hurt anyone to get it, we don't have to manipulate someone else's life, we don't have to pay for it, for we were born with it already embedded within us. All we need to do is activate it. I have come to understand that the one great truth is that all mankind is connected, inseparable from the one great mind. Defined by different names from different mystics, religions, and philosophers, such as Universal Mind, Cosmic Mind, Infinite Mind, Spirit, God-Mind, and God. No matter what you call it, we are expressions of it, the experience lies in that of the individual's innermost mind. Meaning, how you see it, connect to it, etc.

So how does this pertain to power? When you think of it, lack of peace, lack of self-esteem, poverty, fear, etc., all these negative traits exist because we lack the ability to influence positive traits to exist in our minds. We lack the type of power that delivers those things we desire, be it prosperity, courage, or strength. We have not connected to the highest power, Inner God power.

Through the understanding of "Inner God Power" and the application of it, one can eliminate weakness in their being, which prevents him or her from establishing Divine Oneness and experiencing life with peace and prosperity and evolving into a greater being. This lesson will demonstrate that one does indeed have a real power that can be activated through meditations, astral projection, and kundalini awakenings, the manifestation, peace, prosperity, and truly experience oneness with the source or what one may call God.

If all that is weak in a person could be eliminated, the only motion remaining would be the mental motion of success. Everything that one would think or do would d be another step toward succeeding in one's goal but how can one generate a thought positive enough to be successful if the human mind contains energy upon which the habit pattern of weakness is formed?

When an individual learns to contact and release the hidden power of the subconscious mind, he or she can manifest in their lives power, wealth, happiness, and joy. When you learn to apply "Inner God Power," you will be able to break down the duality of mind, identifying its consciousness and subconsciousness. In defining subconsciousness, you need to understand that the mind is the place where seeds grow(thought). If all thoughts planted remain powerful and harmonized, the same outside occurrence will take place in one's life. However, in order to obtain this inner power, one must be diligent in the control of his or her thought process. This process" is termed, consciously co-operating with the infinite power Most people tend to attempt to change circumstances and conditions by working with them, while the real answer is in the cause. (The mind) It is in the way one projects the cause that brings about outward manifestations. The cause molds with Universal Intelligence and generates the outside effects one has before them. It is important to remember that the individual must sincerely believe in this process, keeping the thought of weakness, illness, poverty, etc., out of the thoughts.

Your consciousness cannot and will not participate in reason. Biblically speaking, it has no respect for persons. It resonates with thought; its job is to deliver or respond through generating external manifestations. While the habit of positive thinking may not be the easiest task to perform, it's the responsibility of the thinker seeking change. The one seeking wealth, health, strength, and joy. The power of the subconscious mind responds to fear and positive thought. Thoughts become things; the thinker must make a choice with the full belief of a positive outcome.

Once the mind accepts an idea, execution begins. When the mind accepts thoughts of weakness, lack, evil, etc. the mind manifests these things in one's life...

Thus, your thoughts should remain harmonized at all times. It should be a habitual action of one's daily life. It is very important to understand that the subconscious cannot participate in reasoning. It doesn't stop because the thought you were thinking was evil, thought of anger, etc. Its job is to respond via external manifestation.

The habit of positive thinking is not always easy; however, it is fear that generates negative thoughts, and one way to banish negative thoughts is to banish fear. The power of the subconscious mind demonstrates that everyone has the power to choose and whatever your conscious mind believes to be true, your subconscious will accept it and bring it into manifestation. "Your mind is not evil" You can even heal the body as stated in a very well-known biblical scripture." What things you soever ye desire, when you pray, believe that ye will receive it" (Mark 11:24) This confirms fear can be banished as well as physical ailments, as long as the one praying truly believes it is possible. "But there is only one process of healing, which is faith, for according to your faith it is done unto you. With all of our discussion of mind, the question now lies, as to what is mind? Ernest Holmes, author of "Science of Mind' states that the mind is the first cause. It is the origin of everything. It is Universal Intelligence; it is Spirit or that which we call God. This Universal Intelligence is the life principle that has no respect or persons. It travels through all manifestations. The cause is thought, the manifestations are the effect of the thought. It is neither good nor bad, simply respond to the thought generated. It works for us, by working through us. We must understand that for this power to work, we must recognize it as power. We must remove the limits we set on a principle that is limitless. Simply put, thoughts become things. Holmes as well believes that one can heal everything from weak human characteristics to physical ailments as well., once the mindset is changed with an unwavering belief that power is within, it need not be acquired, simply activated.

Holmes asks the question, 'What breath are we breathing, other than this breath" (page243)

Referring to the breath of God which animates creation with a presence of true divinity…

Dear reader, do not allow your thoughts to dwell on lack of healing but on that which we breath inwardly to activate healing,

"When eliminating human weakness, one must first believe that the God power of your mind is greater than any obstacle before you. You cannot let your mind dwell on failure or frustration and if problems persist, one should go into a deep meditation and raise their consciousness above the mental level of the problem. Thus, proving that human beings do not have to live with human weakness, but when understanding that there is something greater than the situation at hand, the process of inner God power can commence taking place. During the journey, one may surely fail, however, failure is but an alert of telling you which direction to go. Surely if the path you are on is serving you no purpose, you can walk blindly, or you can heed the message that it is time to walk a different path. Failure simply instructs you to go left when one is going right. Go right, and surely you are one step closer to becoming a winner. Embrace the winner's spirit, understanding that praise brings more rewards than feelings of self-pity. In order to keep that winners' spirit, one should never give too much focus on feelings of frustration, fear, and or doubt, one should remain an active individual in his or daily life towards the finish line, one should also believe that the God-power of your mind is greater than any obstacle you may be facing.

Lastly embracing the winner's spirit requires one to think positively rather than negatively and when and if negative thoughts arise, the individual should take him or herself into a meditation state that will lift his or her consciousness or channel his God Power.

One way to channel God's power into your daily activities is by using positive affirmation during meditation before going to bed. "To open up the mind, you must turn inward to the body as a channel and a vehicle for God's power to flow through." When one does this, he or she will be able to see and feel the power of God which will also allow them to see that he or she is not only not alone, but part of something greater.

This feeling of belonging will eliminate things such as fear, lack of confidence, ego, etc. All while helping him or her to eliminate undesirable weak human characteristics. Meditation brings you to the most positive self-image of yourself." Thus, allowing you to eliminate your human weakness."

"The most profound life changes can be found when an individual loves inner perfection above all else. When the need for outward support is diminished, moving closer to the concept of God becomes one's sole purpose." One way to channel God power into you is that you must practice the vigor of habitual contact meditation in order to improve one's chances of developing inner awareness so that one can dissolve human weakness and permanently face God. It is here that the demonstration of constant meditation not only helps change the perception of self but when such an event takes place, you will see yourself in a positive nature, in this capacity, you will begin to feel the presence of inner God power.

This is the experience that aids in the elimination of the human character and allows one to really experience divine oneness with the source we call God. Along with 'contact meditation" you must tackle problems as they arise, not allowing them to fester, but in a calm fashion of self-assurance that no matter what it is, it can be dealt with spiritually. Try to understand the origin of your problem and what you may or may not have done to cause this negative manifestation. Don't dwell on it or fault yourself over it, but rather flow with it, with a knowing that this too shall pass, while focusing on a positive outcome.

Life is but a pendulum, swinging back and forth, nothing

stays still, not even your problems. Thus, the phrase, this too shall pass. The goal is to focus on having a better life, be it affirmations, contact meditations, or acceptance. In the end, this peace that arises from helping yourself have a better life leads to experiencing power in the physical realm, that goal is experiencing the presence of God or Inner God Power.

Another method to experience the presence of God or God's power is by way of astral projection, which is the process of one's spiritual self-leaving its physical self. It can happen voluntarily or involuntarily. It is a vibrational state normal in its occurrence and when accepted and mastered takes you one step closer to personal and spiritual empowerment

"The most important benefit of learning the techniques is that you the student become empowered by having a life-changing experience. You will experience a dramatic change in your awareness and perception of the universe and yourself. Also, you will obtain insights and knowledge of past life issues and overcome many of their fears." In this finding, the obvious is that when you get to the point of life where your self-perception is changed and you see the same of the universe, the result is a positive transformation, from which inner God power begins to take form while eliminating human weakness. The temporary leaving of the body demonstrates that we are more than we realize. That from our inner core(spirit) the truth of human potential can be found. "Another benefit for the out-of-body explorer is that you will know from experience that they are multidimensional spiritual beings. Such beings are not attached to or addicted to realities based on form and substance in this there can be no human weakness, as you are focused on the new awareness of being a multidimensional being.

"When you understand that you are a multidimensional being, you will, no doubt, come to the realization of the potential you possess, such as the ability to awaken the divine energy that we are all born with, yet very few acknowledge or seek its existence." That power is called a kundalini awakening when the kundalini is awakened, she transforms our outlook and makes us see the world around us in a new way. "What seemed difficult now seems enjoyable." This is proof of the beginning of eliminating human weakness, when we can see the lighter side of life, with this vision we can strengthen ourselves. "To understand his or her true self until this Kundalini must be awakened." It is awakened through intense meditation to the Universe or God allowing you to experience a level of bliss in both daily life and internally. "This level of bliss assists the mind into correct thinking when one understands truth and deposits thoughts that are harmonious, this then begins the process of eliminating human weakness." When I was eight years old, my favorite television character was Wonder Woman. She could stop bullets, she could fly, she fought for justice, and she was even beautiful. How awesome could it be to be like her I would think to myself, yet I with all her skills, I believed I could be that beautiful. I would often dream of having powers like her so much that growing up, I became obsessed with having power. Even though I never really knew what it meant. My whole childhood was crushed with moving from home to home and in this journey of being moved around, I saw, I felt, I experienced a lot of pain. My desire for being wonder woman grew stronger as I began soul searching. Who am I? What am I? How can I be strong with all this pain? How can I block the bullets of heartache and how can I be beautiful? After the trauma of my life, by the time I hit forty years old, however, my spirituality began to shake and stir within me as the journey began, and lo and behold it came to me. Beauty was internal, and the outward portion of it was irrelevant for my spiritual growth.

The things I discovered that I didn't like about myself, and my life became my focus. Knowledge was the key, yet wisdom was well hidden. Persistence was key if I was going to be happy. I was not going to be this statistic of the shuffled uneducated woman who dies with an untold story. I would find happiness, I would not be weak, I would not live in poverty. Motherless or Fatherless, I would be more than my circumstance, I would be successful, and I would be powerful. This constant thought I believe, drew the world of metaphysics into my life and I have learned that no matter your background, no matter your weakness or circumstance, past or present, we all have the power, inner power, God power to have all that we desire in life.

We don't have to be afraid of change, or fear of poverty. I have learned that this fear is what keeps those things around. I have learned that we all have the power it's an inner God power in which we were all born with.

I have learned, that while psychological therapy is a good thing, it also prevents us from tapping into to our God power. It allows us to find peace in medicine instead of meditation, it offers us a gateway to addiction of medication instead of addiction to seeking higher consciousness.

If you must sit on a couch and tell someone your issues, remember to add meditation to the process. For you are not your circumstances, you are not your pain, you are not your fears, you are light. A source of frequency taking up space in a physical body. As for me, I found my inner peace and my health when I said Fuck your couch and sat in meditation with higher consciousness as my healer.

THE POWER OF THREE:
THOUGHTS, EMOTIONS, AND WORDS

It is essential to be in alignment with the Universe when you are attempting to be a co-creator. The Universe does not understand whether you're kidding, genuine, or simply talking out of indignation. It's a responder. If you are thinking, attempting to co-create something positive and while you put the thought in your mind, you're upset about what's happening at your place of employment, so much to the point that you can feel your stomach turn, and your heart race, rest assure the Universe is going by the feeling of what's happening at work, not your initial positive thought. Anything that happens from that moment will be based on that vibration.

Every second of everyday a thought is produced in the mind of every man, woman, and child. Even more important, words are expelled and with it comes emotions. Even if you don't intend for it to interface, it does so by natural occurrence. In the last twenty years of spiritually consulting others, I constantly came across individuals who made statements such as "I know thoughts become things, so why can't get what I think about"? I

207

generally ask, "What were you feeling when you were suspecting that idea of want, and what words did you detail in your discourse?" They never remember.

It reacts to the strongest vibration. In short, you get what you focus on. You have to practice matching thoughts with your words and how you feel about the want. Just as you cannot expect bread to rise without baking soda, you cannot expect to have positive thoughts manifested if your thinking doesn't align with your words and emotions. Without this formula, there is no balance, if there is no balance, you might as well get ready for a life of mayhem and confusion.

How would you make a thing in the event that you are not sure of its appearance? The hardest thing on the planet I believe is to remain in alignment with your wants versus your human sentiments. If you think of it, it's like activating a false faith.

Here is a perfect illustration of what I mean. You wake up in the morning excited about going on a job interview, you've been talking about it all week, now that the time has come to claim it, you feel butterflies. During the interview, you are normally nervous, but you survive. You get home and a family member asked you, "Did you get the job"? You reply" I doubt it, I was so nervous, and the assessment test was too hard, I wore the wrong suit, and I was ten minutes late, I feel like I wasted my time, nothing went right.

Notice again, there is no alignment here. This time the words are out of sync. Your desires don't match up. Universal Intelligence will respond to what you focused more on.

This power of three can be seen as a mental transmutation. The reconditioning of the mind to think for itself, based on individual truth. Furthermore, adding belief or faith, demonstrated by emotions and words expelled. As per the New Testament, "Be ye transformed by the power of your mind"

Imagine how much better this world would be if we were all in tune with our first cause, our mind, in this, planting seeds of peace, good health, abundance, love, and every positive condition for every man, woman, and child and living source on the planet. The Universe has no choice but to respond to that which we put out collectively. It is important to remember to see the change for all not just for selfish gain.

The purpose of this dissertation is to show that one's desires are fully manifested through thoughts, emotions, and words combined. Furthermore, the mind is the first that feeds off data from all three elements simultaneously. When this is understood and done consciously, one can create a positive impact in their life as well as society as a whole.

Review of Literature

Why is it that many people have dreams, goals, and wishes, yet many state none of the mentioned are happening? What is it we are missing? Upon understanding the lesson in *"Ask and It Is* "Given, by Abraham Hicks, I came to learn that we are not manifesting our desires because we are holding on to a vibrational pattern that does not match our desires. It's not about where you grew up, you don't need to change your environment, or your circumstances to have what you want, you need only to be a deliberate connector of your consciousness and have a true determination for change. You must be aware of where you are and where you are trying to go. (37)

Yet, how does one know what they are attracting? The perfect answer according to Hicks is if it's something that makes you feel good, then you are attracting good vibrations and goodwill come, if you feel bad about it, then you are not in alignment with your vibrational match and you need to reverse it. How then can you assure that you stay with the right vibrational match? By focusing, on the signs of your feelings teaches Hicks, you can comprehend with total accuracy, all that you are currently living or have ever lived. (29)

By focusing on the manner in which you believe, you can

satisfy your purpose behind being here, and you can proceed with your expected development in the blissful way that you proposed.

"You get what you think about whether you want it or not" (22) Results come forth hence where your thinking lies. I understand now what it means to be a vibrational being, one who sends out signals and receives according to the signals we send. This signal moves immediately from where we are in our now moment. The longer you focus on a particular thing, the stronger the vibration becomes. (39)

"Every thought vibrates, every thought radiates a signal, and every thought attracts a matching signal back. We call that process the Law of Attraction. The Law of Attraction says: That which is like unto itself is drawn. And so, you might see the powerful Law of Attraction as a sort of Universal Manager that sees to it that all thoughts that match one another lineup." (25)

Opportunity from the dread of undesirable encounters will never be accomplished by attempting to control the conduct or on the other hand, wants of others. Your freedom must be permitted by changing your very own vibrational purpose of fascination. Everything happening in our lives we generated based on what we gave our highest focus on because we live in an attraction-based reality. (42)

In any case, when you find out about the Law of

Attraction, and once you know about how your consciousness works based on your emotions, you will no longer be concerned with the possibilities of undesirable results. You will understand that nothing can hop into your experience without your welcome. As well as nothing can keep you from returning to the state of bliss the moment you decide to "feel" your way back in when things are working in your favor. (48)

There are three steps to perform in order to be or have whatever you desire consist of asking, without asking, there can be no answer. It is also the way you ask... Nowadays, there are a few people encountering extraordinary hardships or injuries, and as a result of how they are living at this moment, their asking is in an elevated and exceptional spot. Also, in view of the force of their demand, Source is reacting in kind. What's more, despite the fact that the individual who is doing the asking is normally so engaged with the injury that they are not specifically accepting the advantage of their own asking, future ages—or even current ages who are not, at the present time, prohibiting—are accepting the advantage of that inquiring. As you see, while we started talking about thoughts when it comes to adding the words, the circumstances of one's life, can play a factor of the intensity in the asking, making that thought a negative one, thus Universal Intelligence begins to respond according to the intensity of the negativity. It's not so much about controlling the thoughts as it is about guiding the thoughts with positive emotions, in the end, it makes the words that flow a vibrational match. (49)

The second step to activation required no work on our part at all. It resides in the spiritual realm, it's the listening with belief for the answers. Some call this faith or connecting to consciousness. Either way, the answer is working not from the words you spoke but from the vibration or feeling you had when you asked.

Lastly, feeling the worthiness, or allowing the thing you ask for to enter into your realm. Many times, we ask for a thing and don't believe we will receive it so when it arrives, we don't allow it in. (49)

In discussing the feeling of unworthiness, one of the lessons in "*The Power of Now*. Eckhart Tolle teaches how one can have peace by eliminating negative emotions such as feeling unworthy, by allowing yourself to experience your new moment. For what can the morrow bring with worry.

How would you make a thing in the event that you are not sure of its appearance? The hardest thing on the planet I believe is to remain in alignment with your wants versus your human sentiments. If you think of it, it's like activating a false faith.

Imagine how much better this world would be if we were

all in tune with our first cause, our mind, in this, planting seeds of peace, good health, abundance, love, and every positive condition for every man, woman, and child and living source on the planet. The Universe has no choice but to respond to that which we put out collectively. It is important to remember to see the change for all not just for selfish gain.

"You are the architect of your own life," it is yours to make or to mar. By the power of thoughts, you are building, but if you are not obtaining what you truly desire, perhaps you are not building properly. (3)

Author Henry T. Hamblin, author of *"The Power of Thought."* teaches that thought is a spiritual power, as well as the greatest power accessible to mankind, is the power of thought.

Every nation is in its present state from its collective thinking. Be it peace, prosperity, anarchy, poverty, or murder. Not to say that these thoughts are done deliberately, but more through suggestion. From what we hear, see, taste and even touch. The seed of perception is planted. For example, if a woman or man reads an article on signs to tell if your spouse is cheating, suddenly every small action appears to be a telltale sign of cheating, and your thoughts begin to believe what it thinks it sees and there goes what was probably a great marriage falling apart, all because of a seed of suggestion. Naturally, the mind begins to wander, and the thoughts begin to follow. As you see by this example, the mind can cause you to do many things. Things you might not have done had you been present in your thinking. (3)

How then does this connect to the power of three? Let's take a look at a quote from many such as Mahama Gandhi: "Watch your thoughts, they become your words, watch your words, they become your actions, watch your actions, they become your habit, watch your habits, they become your character, watch your charter, for it becomes your destiny."

The lessons encourage us in that thought is the instrument used to pull in the like just as the unlike, the rich over poor people and powerless over the solid. Be that as it may, the intensity of thought ought not exclusively to be an endless supply of realism. Achievement is something to be thankful for, yet one ought to be aware of turning into its slave. In the event that you don't have power over your life, to the point life will have command over you. Your contemplation ought to be that of administration. How might you have any kind of effect on the planet? As we have just talked about, this should be possible with positive contemplations. From thinking overabundance rather than need, wellbeing rather than ailment, plenitude for all rather than destitution. Subsequently, we should abstain from intuition shameful musings and really train our brains to see a delightful world. (31)

Hamblin makes it clear that this training of thought, while necessary, one would be in error to believe that one can simply change at his or her one will. It takes obedience of Universal

Laws, not demands. Remembering, while selfish request may bear fruit, it is never sweet for long. Thus, training our self to thing thoughts of good will, instead of hate, thoughts on the positive poles, in that we enter into correspondence or state of oneness.

While this may all appear to be dull, remember that purposeful positive reasoning is fundamental for your life as well as the life of everyone around you. At the point when things around you appear to be loaded up with hardship, center around the littler triumphs so as to keep up or acquire an inspirational outlook after all. (37)

As the builder, your tools are your thoughts. This will affect how you feel about the outcome. The brighter the emotion the better the feeling, the more effective choices you can make in the process and in the end, desired results. If you took a moment to reflect on the last time you made a conscious decision, try to remember how you were feeling when you came to the final conclusion. What was the outcome? If you were in a state of anger, then more likely than not, the decision you made was fueled with negative energy and bought with its negative results. How did you feel after all was said and done when you cooled down? Chances are you felt resentful. The term think before you speak is not just a saying, it is an instruction, for when you truly think before you speak, you give yourself, time to cool down if needed, reflect on the feeling at hand and make wiser conclusions, thereby having better results. (38-39) Again connecting the power of three for when the mind receives the right words the proper instructions for that which you desire can be manifested accordingly. This has confirmed the lesson I have come to understand that emotions and decisions go hand in hand. When reading an article *"Emotions and decision" in the Annual Review of Psychology* Jennifer Lerner, discusses, that while we focus on the realm of Metaphysics, we should know that the late great Carl Jung was a psychologist who paved the way for western society to accept metaphysics and some of the works of metaphysic and psychology are one in the same with different wording meaning the same thing (315)

Collectively the authors of that article including Ye Li, and Karim Kassam have unfolded various material from published professionals on the topic at hand. Hence, they have concluded that there are eight themes that in looking over research on feeling and basic leadership, eight noteworthy topics of logical request developed. (For the purpose of this dissertation, we need to look at four of them.) Predictable in that the field is in its first phase, the individuals ordinarily: 1. change with a measure of research conducted, 2. include little contending hypotheses, 3. contain little authoritative determinations, 4. display similar qualities in methods. (5)

Looking at the first subject it suggests that basic feelings impact basic leadership. This theme states your feelings have an impact on how you make decisions, meaning if an individual is uncomfortable with the result of a negative choice, they may simply make a choice based on which is safer to deal with, whereas an individual who is filled with gratitude toward a college in which they graduated from, the likely hood of being open to sending money is regardless of if it affects their personal budget. These examples are the result of making decisions based on emotions that arise based on the situation at the current moment. "Thus, integral emotions degrade decision making as it includes emotions such as fear." Solomon RC. 1993, *Passions, Emotions, and the Meaning of Life (6)*

Theme two; Incidental emotions influence decision making. This theme states that we carry over emotions from previous situations into our current ones. A perfect example is a bad breakup where one individual had a habit of yelling, now in the current situation the new partner yelled, and your next emotion is the same as the original one affecting your decisions thereby your current thoughts. The process is known as the carryover of incidental emotions. Simply put, moving backward emotionally *"(7)*

Theme Three: "Emotions shape the depth of thought." Notwithstanding the substance of thought, feelings additionally impact the profundity of data preparing identified with basic leadership. Similarly, as with other feeling research, early examinations concentrated on the impacts of a positive and negative disposition. Feelings help ideally explore social choices. Researchers have conceptualized feelings as correspondence frameworks that assist individuals to explore and facilitate social connections by giving data about others' thought processes and demeanors, eventually taking into account the creating and maintaining of solid relationships. (9)

In the event emotions serve a multiskilled task through alerting the individual should a scenario need further thinking, requests further thought, they assumed, in that particular moment of negativity the mind should flag risk and consequently increment careful, organized getting ready, and positive temperament ought to flag a protected scenario and cause progressively heuristic getting

ready. To be sure, numerous investigations

have incontestable that people in positive (negative) filled

with feeling states were increasingly (less) compact by

heuristic signals, for instance, the power, allure, or amiability

of the supply, and therefore the length as against the

character of the message; they likewise depended a lot of on

stereotype. (9)

Theme four: Emotions influence interpersonal

decision-making.

"Emotions are inherently social, and a full explanation of

their adaptive utility requires an understanding of their reciprocal

influence on interaction partners. As an example of how complex

such influences can be, people derive happiness merely from

opportunities to help and give to others with no expectation of

concrete gains. (12)

Though interpersonal emotions can influence others'

behavior by communicating information about an emitter's

intentions, they can also change decisions and behavior as a

function of the corresponding or complementary emotional states

they evoke in others. "Anger can elicit fear when communicated

by those high in power (or corresponding anger when

communicated by those low in power" (13)

As you can see from these professionals, emotions do affect your thought process and thus your decision-making. Your emotions (belief system) affect your thoughts (first cause) and your words (your affirmation or declaration) thus affecting what vibrations you send out into the universe, thus how life reacts to your order.

How then does one create positive thoughts as fuel for the mind when there is so much chaos in the world? How can one even have power for that matter? This great answer comes from The *Science of Getting Rich* by Wallace D. Wattles, writing that consciousness is the only real power that will produce tangible things, including riches. Even if the world be chaos, there is a formless substance as he puts it from which all things are formed from. Thus, is everything we see is created out of this formless substance, it is safe to say that there is no chaos in the world, but chaos in the mind and this is where the issues lie. (18)

It was very clear in reading that once you not only understand that what formulates begins with having faith, or a strong belief in what you think to be true. See the world as chaotic, it will be that in your environment. While Wattles is speaking on getting rich, I found its connection to the power of three as he emphasized that in order to have a thing, whatever it is, one must first get right of the old idea of it. Think lack, receive lack etc. Whatever you are planting is the type of fruit you will see. Thus, speaking (words) with negativity (thoughts) and believing it to be so (emotions). (22)

Understanding that the feeling needed in most cases is gratitude, most people, even myself at one point, tend to gravitate towards feeling grateful once the manifestation of their desires has come to past, Wattles teaches it is the gratitude beforehand that helps the manifestation process as the more gratefully we fix our minds on the universal substance, the greater things will come, thus, it adds to our feeling good which is planting the seed for good to continue to flow.(33)

It is the new thought, the good thought of gratitude that brings your consciousness into a place of harmony. Wattles states, "Draw nigh unto God, and he will draw nigh unto you" This he says is a statement of psychological truth." (34).

The thought of man must be done in a certain way, while this phrase at first cause me to think the author meant with faith, as in being certain, what he was saying that the thought must be so clear, so accurate in order to impress this substance, that it may know, exactly what formless should be formed. Thus, accuracy is a necessity in manifesting anything. Wishing isn't sufficient enough, everyone wishes. Your mental statement must be anything but vague.

The mental impression of your desire should remain consistent within the mind. (34)

In Wattles instruction on remaining consistent with positive mental impression for riches or otherwise, (thought) he discussed the use of the will, emphasizing that you should refrain from discussing past pain, (words) be it of a financial nature or not, he elaborates on refrain from going into the darkness of the mind of one's early youth and the troubles that came with it (emotion)

In concurring with all the other authors in this dissertation, Wattles even instructs as to keep your thoughts wholly to riches: ignore the poor. This lesson can be included in with keeping your mind focused upon that which you seek. (47)

Author Neville Goddard of" *Feeling is the Secret,"* teaches us that the world, and all inside it, is man's adapted cognizance externalized. Cognizance is the reason just as the substance of the whole world. So, it is to the awareness that we should turn in the event that we would find the mystery of creation. "No idea can be impressed on the subconscious until it is felt, but once felt – be it good, bad, or indifferent – it must be expressed. Feeling is the one and only medium through which ideas are conveyed to the subconscious." (6)

"Therefore, the man who does not control his feeling

may easily impress the subconscious with undesirable states. By control of feeling is not meant restraint or suppression of your feeling, but rather the disciplining of self to imagine and entertain only such feeling as contributes to your happiness. Control of your feeling is all-important to a full and happy life." (6)

Hence Goddard states, "emotions go before appearance and is the establishment whereupon all appearance rests. "Be cautious about your states of mind and sentiments, for there is a whole association between your sentiments and your obvious world. Your body is an enthusiastic channel and bears the undeniable characteristics of your predominant feelings. Enthusiastic aggravations, particularly smothered feelings, are the reasons for all sickness. To feel strongly about a wrong without voicing or communicating that inclination is the start of sickness – dis-ease – in both body and condition. Try not to engage the sentiment of disappointment or then again disappointment for dissatisfaction or separation from your target results in ailment. (8-10)

Think feelingly just of the state you want to figure it out. Feeling the truth of the state looked for and living and following up on that conviction is the method for all appearing wonders. All progressions of articulation are realized through a difference in feeling. A difference in feeling is a change of fate. All creation happens in the space of the intuitive. What you should obtain, at that point, is an intelligent control of the activity of the inner mind, that is, control of your thoughts also your feelings. "Get into the spirit of the state desired by assuming the feeling that would be yours were you already the one you want to be. (29) As you embrace the feeling of the state you are seeking, you are relieved of all effort to make it so, for it is already so. There is a definite feeling associated with every idea in the mind of every human being. Capture the feeling associated with your realized wish by assuming the feeling that would be yours were you already in possession of the thing you desire, and your wish will objectify itself." (29)

Desires become things when they are given substance with emotions in the Mind.

Thoughts are the motherboard of the Universe. They contain the data that offers structure to our virtual reality. Without inclination or substance, we would not have the capacity to see the thoughtforms in our Mind. The emotions we use to offer substance to the contemplations in our Mind originate from one of two sources: dread or Love. The thoughts we think are given substance with dread-based emotions, for example, outrage, dissatisfaction, or nervousness, will move toward becoming things (genuine life experience) that we experience as "negative" or "terrible".

(www.metaphysics-for-life.com/thoughts-become-things.html)

The thoughts we think are given substance with Love based sentiments, for example, appreciation, harmony, joy, and prosperity, will move toward becoming things we experience as "positive" and "great". For instance, how about we take the thoughtform of "personal finances. We all are giving substance, or feeling, to the thoughtform of cash each day. For a few, this inclination is "insufficient" or "cash is a wellspring of underhandedness". The words "insufficient" or "detestable" are likewise thoughtforms, yet they are given substance in the Mind with dread by nearly everybody.

(www.metaphysics-for-life.com/thoughts-become-things.html)

When we offer substance to the idea type of cash with dread-based sentiments, we make real-life encounters including cash that are additionally given substance with sentiments of outrage, dissatisfaction, and nervousness. It doesn't make a difference how a lot of cash we have or don't have, it will never feel like it's sufficient. Or on the other hand, we may dispose of it since it feels wickedness to us. Then again, when we offer substance to the thought-form of cash with Love-based emotions like appreciation and prosperity then our real-life involvement with cash will likewise be given substance with those sentiments. When we spend or get cash, we feel appreciative. Whatever measure of cash we have, regardless of whether it's a little or a ton, we experience sentiments of prosperity. (www.metaphysics-for-life.com/thoughts-become-things.html)

When we understand that our genuine life experience is truly comprised of thoughtforms given substance by inclination in the Mind, at that point the considerations become less critical. The emotions actually "matter" - or offer substance to our musings._

(*www.metaphysics-for-life.com/thoughts-become-things.ht ml*)

Thus far we understand that what you think connects to what you say and what you say connects to how you feel per our previous reviews. This intention is what is taught by Andy Shaw author of *"Mastering the Law of Attraction."* Simply put you will get what you attract, hence, it is not about knowing that it exists and learning more and more stuff about it. The intention on writing the book is to demonstrate how to achieve real-life results. How then can you get what you want using your words, your thoughts, and your emotions? Shaw teaches that you must "choose" to always be ecstatic within yourself. When you feel yourself getting irritated with yourself for not accomplishing something, not have any significant bearing something, not knowing something, at that point you are to get yourself at the time and stop and think for only a couple of second. Discover the words to acknowledge while turning around the inclination. For instance: I am not content with myself at the present time and that isn't helping me, what's done is done. I am however happy within myself for noticing that I wasn't happy with myself and reversing my thoughts about it. (2)

The "secret is to then create what you desire with your thoughts, have attained a state of mind where you have actually had it happen and felt it happen in your mind, and in that process, you become detached from it, because you already had it. Then what happens is you work diligently on making that a reality for everyone else, as it is already a reality in your mind, and you keep going until you get there." It's about creating with your mind while controlling your thoughts so it can focus without interruption or doubt. All power lies within your mind. The only price you need to pay is to establish the mental equivalent in your subconscious mind. You must give in order to get. The giving is the seed you plant and the belief of its manifestation

It is at this mental state does the demonstration of when the mind is at peace, the words and the emotions all roll in sync

(16-18)

In the book *"Cosmic Energizer, The Miracle Power of the Universe,"* writer Joseph Murphy talks about a vitality inside man. This power, states murphy is the presence of God inside man. The enormous energizer streams amicable, calmly, musically, and happily, through us we are acting in sync and harmony with this energizer, and we will show agreement, wellbeing, harmony, and wealth of the vast in our lives. At whatever point we enjoy regret, self-judgment, hatred, or any type of negative reasoning, the Divine Energy ends up caught inside us and delivers a wide range of inconvenience. (15)

Thus, teaches Murphy, that to reverse the negative vibration, one ought to choose to change the image that lies before them. "Choose to acknowledge the infinite healing power instead of sickness, this is an act of faith, recognizing the only Presence, Power, Cause and Substance. Contemplate." (15) Universal Intelligence from the highest standpoint and claim Divine Oneness, saturate your whole being into it. Decree, that the Universe is silently and constantly healing every cell in your body down to the last atom. Decree even as much as its reproduction of wholeness, beauty, and perfection wherever the imperfection is.

Even in wealth, the cosmic energizer works on the

behalf of the receiver as Murphy tells the profound story of a man during the depression who created play money and declared he was rich. This odd gentleman would do odd jobs to pay what bills he could. However, his drive was for wealth through real estate. He created a game in his basement and people would come over and marvel as well as ridicule him. However, this gentleman would not change his mind or emotion. In the end, his homemade game became a household game we now know as Monopoly. This true story says a lot when you think of it. The gentlemen, in spite of financial circumstances, would not give in to his surroundings. He kept his excitement and intentions high; he spoke of what he was going to be, and, in his heart, he believed it. The vibration he was sending was that of a conscious co-creator, one whose words, thoughts, and emotions made him the most prominent game creator of his time and ours.

In short, when you choose to acknowledge your desires through positive words, thoughts and emotions collectively, as opposed to your current situation, you still see the manifestation. How long does it take? As long as you are in alignment, time should never be a concern. Time is not for you, it's for the Universe. "Dream lofty dreams, and as you dream so shall you become. But be sure to put the foundation of faith and confidence in the Power of God to bring it to pass." (21)

The Cosmic Energizer is also called, Universal Intelligence, Energy, Eternal Light, or God. Either way, the one energizer is your awareness, the I AM or Life Principal. One Energy dividing itself into itself also known as superior and inferior natures or even better, the conscious and subconscious mind. How then, does this connect with our topic of the power of three?

"The conscious mind conveys ideas and images to your subconscious mind, and the latter determines how your thoughts and images become manifested as form, function and experience life." (114)

On the off chance that you have an unfulfilled want, dream, or objective, you might harbor in your mind a few considerations of dread or stress, or you might see obstructions to its satisfaction. Distinguish yourself now with your objective by rationally and sincerely joining with it. Stimulate your optimal in your brain by as often as possible visioning its satisfaction. As you add one block to another in the working of your home, your supported vitality will slowly develop and amplify until your intuitive personality is brimming with the nature of your idea and feeling. As you protect and stay dependable to your vision, Cosmic Energy will move through your mental example and cause your craving to traverse from the cognizant circle of life to the abstract condition of mindfulness or intuitive exemplification.

Secured by a Cosmic Energizer, yet as per author Gregg Braden, we are living in a *Divine Matrix*. This Divine Matrix is the compartment that holds this universe. It is the scaffold between all things and the mirror that demonstrates to us what we have made. Everything in our reality is connected to everything else. We need just to take advantage of the power of the universe itself and consider ourselves to be part of the world, not separate from it. The focal point of our mindfulness turns into the truth of our reality. Feeling is the prayer says Braden, "However, it is less about the actual words we use and more about the feeling they create within us" (84)

To just say that we pick another truth isn't sufficient, to pick a quantum probability, we should turn into that method for being by deserting ourselves to the new plausibility and in our new love for that state. The feeling is the language that addresses the Divine Matrix. Feel as though your objective is practiced and your supplication is as of now replied. Remember, no inclination will do, you should grasp the inclination that will make without inner self and judgment. Braden accentuation that the base of our negative encounters might be decreased to one of three all-inclusive feelings of trepidation or a mix of them. relinquishment, low confidence, or absence of trust.

We should progress toward becoming in our lives the things that we experience as our reality. However even before this to occur, one must trust that they have the ability to make such a change. "We can't solve a problem in the same level of thinking that created it, Similarity, we can't change a reality if we remain in the same consciousness that made it"

In reviewing the Divine Matrix, it clearly demonstrates that this force is an energy or as other authors have called it vibration. Either way, its purpose is to bring forth. What it brings forth is entirely up to you. You have the power to choose what you put out in the form of words and emotions and what you allow into your consciousness. It is these ingredients that determine the physical manifestations in one's life. (86-87)

Understand that life is something you the participant must give meaning to. You are the co-creator. According to Daniel M. Jones, author of *"Become the Force,"* it is our responsibility to be the force itself. While this book discusses what Mr. Jones terms as Jediism. Jediism is simply emphasizing on the inner calm, positive thinking, and doing. Jones also states that the force is simply a metaphor for spirit. What metaphysics would call, Universal Intelligence? The goal here is to become a Jedi Master, which would be for this topic one who has mastered life by starting with your thoughts. Assuring that it is creating good vibrations by choosing positive and peaceful thoughts and following it up with positive and peaceful actions.

It is the waking up your mind to think more clearly by deep breathing and positive thoughts, paying close attention to your surroundings to ensure they are not infecting your vibrations. Jones quotes Buddha in saying" I think therefore I am" (47) explaining that while science may say thoughts begin in the brain, the spiritual perspective is that thought is a manifestation of energy the creates what you experience or perceive. (49)

In order to master these thoughts, it is stated to frequently direct your thoughts entirely to what you want to manifest in your life. Simply put, make it a daily habit to declare your intention. Being focused gives you power. Another method Jones focuses on it talking to oneself, yet without criticism. Self-criticism is not the real you. It is only alive because while you aim to think positive, negative self-criticism causes you to manifest negative results and your thoughts and your words, are not on the same page. (50)

It is essential in becoming one with the force, that one learns to control his or her emotions. (Because you are the force aka vibration) Without emotional management, one comes in contact with the dark side of the force (negative vibration).

However, facing that dark side is essential, because through it we learn which emotions don't serve us and in this, we evolve. You are responsible for defending yourself against this negative vibration. Here is s self-defense tactic to assist in staying on track. (51)

That self-defense can come from many sources such as meditation, martial arts, prayer, and yoga. Hence, in all these tactics mentioned, thoughts, words, and emotions are the essential tools to work them. (156). While we discuss the power of three, using words, thoughts, and emotions to manifest our desires, this is not to state that we will not have moments of failure.

While being positive can be a challenge in this day and age, Uell S. Anderson, author of *The Key to Power and Personal Peace* states, "You must right now convince yourself that evil is an effect, not a cause." Evil is the result of erroneous thought conception. Erroneous thought conception is the cause of evil. Evil is a circumstance: and you, as divine part of the universal intelligence, need never be the result of circumstance. (6)

You create the circumstance. Only when you believe circumstance to be greater than you are, will you allow it to continue to develop in your experience. You must allow the Subconscious Mind to create your desires into actuality. For example, if you desire money, let it be an assurance, a conviction that the law must resolve. Then without a doubt, the money will be yours. However, it is important to that you cannot vacillate about it. Don't complain or discuss lack, then in order to make yourself feel good because you haven't seen it manifest yet, make statements that you don't care if have a lot. This is a see-saw effect in the eyes of the universe; thus, nothing will happen. There is a balance of complaint and lack of desire. The result, no money manifestation at all. (9)

This type of balance normally occurs when one works with man-made law and spiritual law at the same time. The negative prompters become activated in the subconscious mind leaving one to believe and or accept lack of sickness and poverty. It is your duty to control these prompters. These prompters are your "words." (10)

You must control these prompters, or they will control you. Through conscious mediation on the spiritual laws of the universe, plant into the Subconscious a conditioned response for good which will automatically displace all negative prompters. The circumstance that has manifested was created from false thought habits which in turn created those negative prompters that you have allowed to be locked in your subconscious.

The subconscious teaches Anderson, is the great creator and it creates exactly what it is prompted to create. (11)

The power of those words(prompters) comes from the level of your faith in the desire.

Faith is nothing other than a sustained effort to impart to the Universal Subconscious Mind that thought which you wish to be manifested in your experience. It means refusing to accept any negative circumstance or to even entertain thoughts of negativity. Faith is complete reliance and trust in the power and greatness of the Universe and absolute truest that whatever you conceive with conviction will be returned to you in this world. The power of positive thinking is limitless according to Allen. "He who banishes negative thoughts from his mind is caught up in the entire expanding power of the Universe" (15)

Let's take a look at why most people think negative in the first place. Usually,

it's from fear or lack of confidence in one's ability to accomplish a thing. So, they project out their feelings using common phrases like," it will never work" "they don't want you to succeed" "that's just the way it is." All this to say, I am afraid I won't be able to be successful in what I desire. (14)

According to Norman Vincent Peale, of "The Power of Positive Thinking," It is important to believe in your abilities. "Without a humble but reasonable confidence in your own powers, you cannot be successful or happy." (6) Any thought of self-esteem affects the process of aligning with your desires and its manifestation. The moment you understand the importance of faith in yourself, or your situation is the moment you begin to acquire an internal peace. With that peace comes to power. It is that mental attitude that is the secret of obtaining success as well as a harmonious life. (6)

An essential strategy to work towards a positive mental frame of mind is to discharge the psyche. Expelling all considerations of abhor, uncertainties, second thoughts, blame and fears. Remember, discharging the psyche isn't the best way to keep an inspirational frame of mind, since once exhausted, the brain can be an unsafe spot. It must be loaded up with something in its place, something positive, something, solid and innovative. Something that when negative vitality comes around, the sign on your psychological outlook peruses "involved." (8)

It is important and even conceivable to keep a substance dimension of vitality. Indeed, even nowadays pressure. How we feel truly affects how we really feel physically. On the off chance that your mind reveals to you that you are drained, the body system, the nerves, and the muscles acknowledge the reality or perhaps that your mind is strongly intrigued, you can keep on at a movement inconclusively. By providing dispositions of confidence to the brain, it can expand vitality. Positive vitality. It causes you to achieve huge action by recommending that you have sufficient help and asset of intensity. Let us be clear if we haven't already to state that the only one who decided how happy you will be is ultimately you. (89)

Like many authors mention, Peale, being no exception, I began to notice many of these techniques of thinking, feeling, and speaking, all seem to stem from a spiritual source. From source energy to vibration, to Universal Intelligence, thus power to have, to be or to do, lies within, that if we can believe, nothing is impossible. Understanding that the way to believing begins with the attitude (emotion) affirmations (words) and the mind (thoughts). Nothing is in your way, lest it be you by thinking thoughts of defeat. Hence being fearful considered defeat, lacking self-confidence is thinking defeat. You cannot have a defeated attitude and expect to experience the harvest. (91)

Discussion

When I was just shy of fourteen years old, I came across a woman sitting on a bench, she was crying. I was simply going to get a quart of milk as instructed by one of my many mothers. Something made me stop to stare. (I realize now it was Universal Intelligence already at work) Words came out of my mouth without my consent as I found myself asking" Why are you crying"? She looked at me with parental eyes and told me to mind my own business and that she was talking to God, not to me, and to leave her alone. "Well God can't hear you because you're crying to loud" You're supposed to be happy knowing you're going to get what you want. "You're confusing him," and with that, I walked away.

It is in times of sorrow just like that woman on the bench, we must remember to be the co-creator, to have the unwavering trust of the Universe to the point that tears of joy replace tears of sorrow. Everybody knows about thoughts becoming things and thinking before we talk, however, there is a distinction in knowing and applying. Our reality has been so dynamic in self without understanding that self is the thing that acquired division a plane where we are altogether associated

We were all born with tools that allow us to pay attention to our emotions and help us balance them. They are tools we use every day. They are sight, smell, touch, taste, and hearing. Before we discuss the fifth tool which is intuition, let's review the first four. How many times have you smelled something foul? Normally, it makes your stomach turn, you may even gag, and the next thing you know you utter something like, "I feel like I am going to be sick" suddenly you're bringing up last night's dinner. This phrase or statement of truth is you putting thoughts and emotions into action. Do you see how it works together? Your senses smelled something, it affected your physical self, it places a thought in your mind and the result was manifested via regurgitation. Now, let's go into the most powerful and overlooked tool, your intuition.

This powerful tool is a vibration that cannot be seen, but it can be felt. It sets off warnings to the brain and the body to let you know something isn't quite right. Pay attention the next time you are walking down a street and feel as if something isn't right, something in you says turn left and you may not even be sure why, but you do, suddenly you hear on the nightly news that there were an incident and people were injured. Your intuition is the Universe's way of guiding you for your betterment and safety. Pay attention to it.

This Something is as simple as a positive word, wrapped in a positive emotion can generate everything we desire. When you ask, how can you have what you want? You have to believe enough to know that the answer is up to you. Beginning with a positive feeling of being worthy of having that which you desire. That is what is meant by such as a man thinketh so is he. The power is there. You have the ability as the I AM to add positive words that generate positive emotions to connect to your thoughts so that the sentence defines your truth.

It is in the application of words, the controlling of emotions that places the image in your mind, in turn, you get as Abraham Hicks says:" What you focus on"

As we have quite recently perused, we have a power that we disregard. Regardless of whether we ignore it because of molding, dread, or essentially the absence of information, this power has been known as The Force, Universal Intelligence, Vibrations, Energy, Spirit, and Cosmic Energy. Regardless of the name, it's basic to perceive this power without dread. Think about every one of the occasions you have reacted in displeasure; how did your day go? What was the aftereffect of the indignation? Did you get what you needed? Presently contrast it with when you reacted in adoration or possibly calmly, what was the reaction? How did you feel inside?

The reason   I am making this inquiry is for the individuals who wonder how to change the recurrence of a negative minute. Hence, on the off chance that you don't care for what your inclination, change it by changing your mindset of it. Making inquiries like what's the most exceedingly terrible that could occur, at that point be appreciative that that isn't what occurred.

Keep in mind, this division is why there is so much pain in the world. When you think lack, you are not just affecting your life, but others around you and across the world. That force that we discussed that has so many names, carries with it your vibration. The slightest emphasis on poverty, sickness, heartbreak, hate, and any other word that is the opposite of a positive pole, gets planted into your mind and the hearers of your words.

The level of toxicity that comes with negative feelings as we have read and I am sure even you have experienced, carries the burden of how good or bad your day or the day of others can go. When you speak, there are other ears that hear you, even if you are not speaking to them, they carry your vibration if they are in a sufficient distance to receive what you are saying. How many times have you shared news with a person good or not so good, and they shared it with someone else? Words and opinions are added on to what you uttered, sometimes more likely than not, they were uttered by naysayers. So, if one utters negative words regarding what they heard about your statement, goals, or aspirations with enough sincere emotion, the universe responds. Hence not in a great way for you, since the words, thoughts, and emotions were from a negative place of the speaker.

This is because the Universe has no respect of persons, giving no concern it, the naysayer had good intentions on your behalf or not. This is the same way negative things happen around the world such as poverty. Too many voices speaking life into something in agreement and sometimes at the same time, such as when millions tune in to the nightly news. Emotions or rage, anger, and lack all sending up signals to the Universe to give that information spoken of, life.

We are one, we have a right to peace, prosperity, and health. We also have the power of choice, we must choose to pay attention to thoughts, or as Tolle states, be a presence in our now.

Surely it takes practice, however, if you were blessed enough to see a new day, that means Universal Intelligence is give you time to try again. The most important thing to remember in this power of three concepts is that no one can do it for you, even though it affects everyone around you, you must hold yourself accountable to make the shift of awareness, verbally, emotionally, and consciously.

When we were children, that very first step we took excited our parents. Imagine the frequency you can send into the world by taking the first steps to be proactive in your thinking, your choice of words, and your emotions. Every day a child is born, it knows all truth until it is plugged into this virtual reality called life. This process is not as hard to perform. It's simply a matter of going back to the beginning. To that place of silence that existed before the rush of one's life started.

Indeed, if you consciously, took the time to be still, and think nothing so that you can focus on how you feel, is the starting point of increasing positive frequencies, cosmic energies, vibrations, and forces. Every author we have discussed, all agree by their writings that words, emotions, and thoughts, must be changed for the better as one affects the other, as well as the manifestations it delivers. Thus, there is no changing your mind, without changing your emotions and there is no changing your emotions without changing your words, and there is no changing your words, without changing your thoughts.

The endless circle of thoughts, words, and emotions is what makes the world go around. Which end of the pendulum we end up on is up to you. Swing upward into positive bliss using positive words to create positive feelings and thoughts and be a happy candidate in your life or swing lowly with negative words, feelings and thoughts and be filled with internal chaos, fear, and other negative storms and experience a life of pain and confusion.

You are the co-creator.

"The personal subconscious as already stated is in the memory bank of the mind. Here over a period of time, a thought accumulation builds, an accumulation of both positive and negative failure thoughts in the mind" (Volume 2 Masters Module page 22) The cognizant and relating subliminal mental demeanor and thought aggregation turns out to be exceptionally imperative as far as wellbeing, because of the way that the individual intuitive impacts the sensory system. Thus, the sensory system influences the non-intentional interior organs, organs, science, and vitality factors all through the body.

Not only do negative and destructive thoughts affect your personal life, but your health as well. The mind affects the body, and the body affects the mind. Another method to counterattack negative thinking is through the use of meditation and the use of positive affirmations. Statements such as I AM, I will, I have, I am grateful, I love, etc.

The practice of conscious mind control can be obtained even with Hatha Yoga, and while it covers the seven psychic centers or chakras, one can find peace in its performance allowing one to embrace more positive feelings, which allows more positive words and alas more positive thoughts. Furthermore, the mind is the first cause, in that it feeds off data from all three elements simultaneously. When this is understood and done consciously, one can create a positive impact in their life as well as society as a whole.

The Beginning of the Power of a Woman

We have all been to that point where enough was enough. If you haven't, consider yourself to be blessed. For those of you who have, you understand that when life gives you lemons and your conscious instruct you to make lemonade, but you don't have the ingredients to do so, it's a disastrous and emotionally painful feeling.

Yet, even when we are at our lowest points in life, the Creator comes into us to show us a way out. Either by way of a person, a phone call, or even better, a thought. I pulled the trigger three times as I cursed God, yet the bullet wouldn't leave the chamber. It was then the question came to me. "Was this the only way out of my situation?" A voice within began to disclose all types of epiphanies into my mind to the point I could feel my body trembling.

Questions raised in my mind at a fast past, so fast, there wasn't enough time to evaluate them let alone ask if they were my own or
God's. Then the final question jumped ahead of all

249

other thoughts and dropped a bomb on me. "How did you get here?" That my friends will be the most painful question you must answer as I did. I blamed everybody. My dad for leaving my mom. My mom for leaving me. My attacker for raping me. My husband for abusing me and cheating on me. It was everyone else's fault.

And lo and behold the question that followed was" Why is anyone else responsible for your actions?" That was the real question, the question I didn't know how to answer because there was no answer other than the one, I fearfully didn't want to answer. I had to answer in truth that although things might have happened to me because of various events, I was responsible for my actions after the fact. Like the clouds on a rainy day separating in both directions, the sun came out in my heart. Strangely enough, holding myself accountable made me feel lighter. Laughing aloud I asked myself, how could that be possible to feel so good at blaming myself?

What nonsense is this? Yet as I began to really think long, hard, and true, I understood. Running to my bedroom to get a notebook and pen (I always write, since I was a child, it made me feel free) and began to analyze my life. I found several

"Powerful action steps "that had I done would have saved me a lot of pain. I decided I would start doing those powerful action steps while I am alive. Now over twenty years later I am still doing it and I tell you this.

Although I started with no money, no friends, and no love I made it. The journey was long and painful, yet I am God's greatest masterpiece and I know that now and every day I make sure my life reflects that which I am. This my sister is what I want to share with you. You are also God's greatest masterpiece, and to avoid sounding like I am male bashing, I will say this, they don't want you to know "how to activate your power".

Because if you did, the truth is 'THE GAME

WOULD BE OVER"

One of the questions I used to ask, and I am sure you ask it too, was, "what is my purpose?"

The answer is simply this in my opinion" Create your own Legend and enjoy the experience until the next birth.

Wherever that birth may be.   Over the next several chapters, I will share with you the action steps that equip me with activating my own power so that you may activate yours as well. I will not be as pleasant in some parts. It may even sound as if I am being harsh with you. Make no mistake my friend, I am. It's sugarcoating your life, that got you here.

What Are You Made of?

In the beginning was the word, but before the word,

there was a thought generated by an infinite,

indescribable force that set the world and the breathing

things in motion.

All things were formed in this process.

Through this process all things are one.

Everything is connected. You are connected to this

indescribable force, and you therefore have a portion of

its power. Even in the tablets written centuries ago, it

was told to you that you have the power to cast out

serpents and scorpions. You are a more than a woman,

you are the giver of life, the Indescribable greatest

masterpieces.

You have the power to bring into the world, life.

You have the power to take away life.

You have the power of intuition which is the Indescribable voice". It is this voice that you are to listen to in times of trouble, worry and confusion. This voice given to you at birth to guide you into a world that give you peace. A world that only need be true for you and you alone. What happens? How did we disconnect from this power and suddenly tuned into the voice of mere men? Could it be that our opposition saw such power and felt intimidated? Perhaps.

Or could it be that we were so focused on the sweet taste of the fruit in which our mother sister took a bite of and succumbed to pleasures. Either way, we must go back, way back. Back into the days of when woman listened to her creator. That infinite, indescribable thing so that we may plug into our intuition and find our way to unconditional love, indescribable peace, and forever flowing abundance. We must allow ourselves to believe having power is not a bad thing. It's a birthright, one that comes with responsibility in its usage.

You have been told that a man's word is his bond, he is held by what he says. People expect him to follow through to those very words he has spoken. We take this lesson to heart; we make agreements based on. When you get married and you both say I do your expected to follow through with those oaths.

When a person at the check-out counter tells you the amount you must pay, they expect to receive that amount. Nothing less is acceptable.

When you're cooking and you have certain ingredients that must be added, if you omit just one, the outcome will be something other than what you have expected. Words and actions go hand in hand; one without the other brings about the result that is almost always not what you desire.

The point here is that the words you use have power; the actions you take allow this power to manifest. You cannot say "I believe" my bills will get paid, and then turn around and tell your friends you have so many bills you don't know what to do. You cannot spend countless hours in worry while thinking it's going to get better.

In this you send conflicting messages to the very source (GOD) (UNIVERSE) that you

are putting your out request to.

Jesus said it perfectly when he" said ask and it shall be given unto you". You have a God given right to ask for a thing with the highest of expectations that nothing short of your desires will come to play.

So why aren't your dreams manifesting? Why are you

still in the same position today that you were in yesterday? You are in the same position today because you are still using yesterday's method for today's result. I know most of you are probably saying, I already know all of this, some of you may even say your pastor tells you the same thing. Well, here is the difference.

I am about to show you how to live in the 'presence" of your world, plug into your God-givenpower and help you remove your fear.

That very source of what is holding you back. But, before we travel these roads, you must get in alignment with your inner self. Thus, follow this book from its beginning to end to get the full benefit. You must be able to be in control with your inner self to connect to the Creator.

Action Step

If money was not an issue. What would your life be like right now? What are the types of friends you would have? Where would you live? What would you do? Take a moment before you read any further to honestly write down, exactly what kind of life would you have. Be free and limitless in your planning.

As a woman, you possess an energy that is craved by the opposition. This energy is so powerful that was even used as a bargaining chip to unite powerful families.

And even in some era's it has been traded in for mere dozens of sheep, goats and cows. Do we too still believe that what lies between our legs is something that should be given away so freely? Should we also follow the trend of serving up even the smallest piece of its value is acceptable behavior? I say no. What say you? However, due to our endurance of pain and underdeveloped recognition of value, we have subconsciously given this energy away.

What lies between your legs is more than an essence of passion? It is your God space, the place where life is form and souls lie in rest for a period. This womb that lives within it, needs every bit of nourishment it can get. Allowing a multitude of hungry life forces to come and go without purpose is risking the life you are preparing to create at the appropriated time.

For the opposition, the experience of orgasm is surely a good feeling, however, it is also the release of energy. Thus, why most men are exhausted after the fact and tend to go to sleep. The woman, however, is a different story. The orgasm of a woman is not only the body reacting to outside stimuli. In the practice of Tantra: just before the climax if you stop and put your attention on the location of your body that needs healing or if you focus your attention on a specific desire. That energy that is being generated in and around your "Charkas" are guiding said energy to do as you will it to do.

Whether you are a spiritual person or not. Your energy is still forming. What you do with it, I believe, can have a huge impact on your way of thinking, feeling, and manifesting in your life. So, the next time you decide to offer the key to your golden gate, make sure it has a purpose other than physical satisfaction. You are much bigger than you realize.

Action Step

There's nothing smarter than a woman who does everything with intention.

Before you have that next sexual encounter, I want you to think of what types of changes you would like in your life. Your health and your present.

Name a few things you need The Creator to help you resolve. Be it in your spirit or your health. Then the next sexual encounter, choose only one of the things (only one at a time, to stay focused) and focus on it while you're reaching your peak. In your mind, be thankful for that thing you desire. If it's your health, picture the area that needs healing and focus on it. Imagine it healed and during that moment, start thanking The Creator in your heart and in your mind. Embrace it, believe it, and watch for the manifestation.

Mental Obligation

Growing up, little girls where told what was expected of them. Learn how to cook so you can get a husband. Keep a clean house, so you can keep a husband.

Lay on your back frequently, because he is, your husband. Get a good education, so you can get a good job. Then as the sign of the times began to change, the new word of wisdom was to start a business, train to become an entrepreneur. We fell into the latest fashion trends to look the part. We even read a few books from the successful to help us stay empowered.

We went out and participated in every 'Women's Empowerment Conference" and leave with a "I can't wait till it's my turn" mindset. All this is fine, however, there is a lesson that was so imperative for success in business, relationships, and personal development that we were not taught on purpose! This lesson would have created a world much different than the one we are in now. So, what is this lesson and why weren't we taught about it? The lesson is "Thinking for ourselves" and the reason we were not taught it was to stifle the growth of the masses so that only the selected few would be in power. As the years went by, the lessons we're being taught by the already successful for a price. A price everyone was willing to pay.

For who doesn't want success? Who doesn't want to be pain free? When I discovered the lesson, I first questioned it. I dissected it, then I put it back together and began to use it. As I watched my life do a three sixty degree turn around, I began to lose friends, questioned by family, and looked at as a woman too arrogant for her own good. Mind you, these stigmas came from those who had yet to reach a level of success and were still hurting from the past.

So, in my efforts to get every woman out of

"that place" I will share that lesson with you.

The lesson is "Thinking" but it's not just thinking, heck we

are all thinking. The lesson is thinking in a "certain way"

That "certain way" thinking is what removes pain, delivers

focus, and allows the thinker to reach their own truth. You

see the school; the church and the politicians all want us to

believe every spoken word. When we are hurting, we seek

healing, so we listen, cry and repeat. Every day, every

week and wait eagerly for the next moment to get that

"feeling" of it's going to be ok. And for a few days we are

ok.

Let me get a bit personal with you but understand what I

say is from love and I had to ask myself the exact same

questions, so please don't receive this as

an attack.

Did it ever occurred to you that you could go straight to

God itself, and get your answers? Did it ever occur to you that perhaps you already have the answers to the questions you are seeking, yet somehow, you feel the answer either wasn't good enough or even worse, you know what you need to do but fear has you too afraid to move? Women dominate the church and the classrooms, all seeking answers that have already been given. So where am I going with this? Everything you have been taught for the most part was not so you could use if or life, who really needs fifteen hundred hours of history, liberal arts, or black history to build a business or work retail or any field for that matter. The history of education was never about teaching you to learn, it was about training you to think their way. Ask yourselves how many times did you say, well if it's in a certain book it must be true? How much do you question your life, the people in it, or even your actions for that matter? Thinking has become something we do on a regular basis, but it's the way we are thinking that is stunting our growth. You have an obligation to break down, question, and arrive at what feels right for you, the reader. Remove yourself from the dogma that forces you to believe what you hear, and ask yourself, how do you feel about what you just heard. If you have questions go to a quiet place and write down that question, ask it aloud and sit in stillness uninterrupted and wait for 'The Creator" to answer it. If you really want to know if something is true, ask yourself, how you "feel" about it. In that if it doesn't sit right internally, chances are more likely than not, you shouldn't receive it. You have an obligation to

'question, analyze, think, feel and rethink, before you accept anything, just because it's written in a book. You have an obligation to "create" a life that is true for you, not a life that women are

"expected" to live. You have an obligation to

"release all those negative images that come from being molested, being raped, or being battered.

It's one thing to "share" your story so that others can grow, but how can another woman grow from your story if they still see your pain. You have an obligation to condition your thinking into "releasing pain. What's so important in "Thinking a certain way" is that The Creator" has given you a power of intuition, for the purpose of seeing truth in such a way that you can have a life of love, peace and prosperity and my dear sisters, when you don't tap into it because you're so busy thinking the way others train you to thinking through conditioning tools like, reality to shows, education, television, "some" churches, media, friends, family, etc. you allow your intuition to be "turned off" and you begin thinking like the masses. Your life then becomes like those things you think of. This is also why it is said, you become like the five people you hang with most. It is also why many say a person is the way they are because of their environment. However, you have an obligation to reach for more if what lies in front of you doesn't make you feel good. That's where The Creator comes into play. I don't care if you live in the south side of east hell. Every human being is offered the opportunity to hear The Creators voice, telling them something isn't right. It's at that moment, your obligation must step up and question, analyze, think, feel then act. No exceptions. There are people in this world who understand that, and because they crave power, they keep your mind busy so that there is no time to "think for your truth" But you know now don't you? So now what? Now is when everything that comes into your path, every person, every activity, every desire, every positive or negative feeling, must be broken down and the decision must be made by you and only you on is this "true "for you. Is this beneficial? Let your intuition work for you, not against you. It's your power, it's your right. Take a moment and be truthful with yourself and your use of sexual energy.

How much energy have you used? For future reference, what power thought or healing will you focus on during the next orgasmic moment. Write it down, keep it to yourself.

The Time Is Now

If ever there has been a time to embrace the power of womanhood, now is it. For way, too long have we allowed the stereotypes of what we should do, be or live dominate the perfection that was originally placed for our existence in the precious moment of our creation. Have you ever felt that something in you was missing? That there was so much more to what you should be doing, or even having for that matter? That feeling my sister is conditioning wearing off and the spirit of truth attempting to find its way to your mind. That my sister is God, The Creator, or whatever you choose to call your ultimate source, whispering in your heart to gain your attention.

The question now is, are you listening? Your belief system was created by man, not you. You have been living another person's truth. If it were not so, you would not have to question your life. It would feel right, not only would it feel right, but life would be right. I remember my son asking me at the tender age of five how is it that his teacher said Christopher Columbus discovered America if there were already Indians on it? The wisdom of the youth is under estimated, for even a five-year-old knew that wasn't logical or true, yet to get a good grade in that class he would have to pretend he agreed with the systems version of "truth" I believe every soul is given wisdom within the womb, how else would we know when it's time to come out, and how to get out said womb. But man, in its effort to control and keep power decided it would create a system that told us who we were before we were old enough to ask the question. Women for example were possession. From bible days to the twentieth century. Give my father a few herds or goats and I am all yours, marry one wife, and keep a bunch of sidekicks (concubines) and you can do it in my face and the law says

I have no say. If I get a side piece,

I may be stoned or labeled an adulterer and force to wear

an "A" on my chest in the while walking through the city

streets. However, our sisters all over the globe are waking

up to the fact that we are some bad mama Jama's with a

level of excellence. Many women have awoken to their

give "Power", and you can tell by the lives they live.

Women like Oprah Winfrey, Maya Angelo, Michell

Obama, even in other countries women like Folorunsho

Alakija, who by the way is worth over $1.9 billion. These

women understand struggle, they understand pain, but they

did not let that be an obstacle.

Instead, they progress despite the pain, the violence, and

the heartbreak, that is what you must do. And that's what I

aim to teach you in this book. Now I may not be worth

$1.9 billion, but with everything in me, I am declaring my

millions here and now. For I understand how the mind works and I know it's doable. Follow me and keep watching. Then add your name to the list of The Power of a Woman. Women are the nurtures amongst the toxic strategies that long to keep us bound. Fear has set in amongst even the law makers, egos are rising like famine in a desolate wasteland. Stand up my sisters, this is your time. A time when you show the world that you matter, that you have value, that you are a necessity not a choice and that you demand equality and are willing to settle for nothing less. It is time to show the world that you are more than a phenomenal woman, but a phenomenal woman with value. You are God's greatest masterpiece with the highest purpose deserving nothing less than every good thing, every ounce of respect and love to be planted at your feet.

Like many words, when we don't fully understand its true meaning, we take away the value.

Power is one of those words. Power to most people is getting money, having statues and a million likes on social media. While those are all cool things the real powerful people like, Bill Gates and Donald Trump, Oprah Winfrey, Beyoncé, and Jay Z, all know the real definition of Power and the make no excuses for acquiring it. Power is: The capacity or ability to direct or influence the behavior of others or the course of events.

That's it, nothing more, nothing less. And that's a mouthful. Now that you understand that what is it in your life, that you have no influence over, what situations require a 360degree turnaround? I am sure there are a lot of things you'd like to change for the better and the first thing we must attack is your mindset. That's right, before you go on a splurge of trying to gain power, you must clean your

mind of all the toxic waste that's' been planted in there.

Either by you or your past or maybe even your

present.

Either way it's got to go.
Over the next few chapters, you will read and learn how to

get this power activated starting with

Acceptance,

Accountability, Prevention, Strategic Thinking, and finally

The Game Plan Action steps. This is book that requires,

action or

your part.

More than reading but participating and following through.

From it you will transform into an Alfa Woman, one who

conquered against all odds, on who has activated her power

and it shows.

Take an honest reflection and ask yourself, what Power moment would you like to create? What in your life would you like to influence for the betterment of your personal life, career, and health? Be honest, write it down.

Acceptance

Before we play in what "Power" can do, understand that the most important step we must engage in is "acceptance" You see, right when I was ready to end my life, I was raised with a series of questions that caused me to think twice. 'Why was I in this mess?" Now, I am not instructing you to go into your past and fill your heart with pain in sorrow. What I am instructing you to do is accept it. Why? Become the past cannot be changed and no amount of therapy can turn the clock and undo the incidents. It happened and questioning whose fault it was or placing blame will not change it.

But, when you can openly say, I was raped, but I am ok, I was in a domestic violence relationship, but I am ok, I had a horrible childhood, but I am ok, is when you have the "power" to move forward.

Understand this, my fellow sisters, you are ok! You only think you are not ok because you keep going back to that dark place that imbedded pain and that pain has been sustained you so much to the point it gave you a false sense of worthiness. Are you breathing? Then you survived.

Now it's time to conquer. How do we conquer. We take control of our "emotions" For it is the emotion that keeps you in depression. Did you know that it is the simplest of things that work, that mankind fears? Why because we can't believe a solution is just that simple. I promise you I was one of those people. I couldn't get past the past. I couldn't get past the pain. Until I realized that the reason, I was hurting was because of how it made me feel inside about myself, and I couldn't stop hurting because of how it made me feel inside about myself because I kept "thinking" about it. And I kept "thinking" about it, because? There is the million-dollar question. Why are you thinking about it?

Why are you giving it fuel? The answer is you're thinking about it because you allow your surroundings to be that it was in your own life. For example, if you're a woman who's survived domestic violence, why would you watch a movie that depicts such an event. Do you realize that you replant the seed of pain every time you do that? Stop doing that! If you're a woman who survive sexual assault why are your eyes stuck on a miniseries where a woman is always getting assaulted? It sounds so crazy I'm sure but ask yourself what is television? You just said it; tell the vision" You are allowing something as simple as media to plant seeds in your head. Ok, so you met a guy that you thought would change your life forever. He did, just not the way you were hoping for. That's' ok, you still have you and no one will ever love you the way you deserve to be loved until you love yourself first. The first way to demonstrate your love to yourself is to accept your past by acknowledgement and disposal. There is no need to hold on to it or revisit memory land when we see our lives being portrayed on the big screen or a new song that just sold a billion. If it reflects what you are trying to leave behind, don't entertain it through engagements. We've been doing that for years. You must condition yourself to understand and believe, that while you may not have any accountability on what happened to you, you have a responsibility to control how you allow it to

make you feel. I will repeat that for you like this. It's not about what happened to you in the past, it's about how you're allowing it to make you feel right now.

Acceptance and accountability go hand in hand. Remind yourself daily that you can make yourself better by changing your feelings.

So now, what can you do to change your feelings, change what you're thinking about.

How do we change our thinking? Find a positive happy thought to replace a painful negative thought.

Then next process of this step is letting it go.

As you continue to read this book, you will probably have already placed doubt into your mind. Why? Because you have been through so many things that you don't expect anything better to come your way. You may even believe you deserve no better than what you have. Your hidden secrets of rape, molestation, drug addiction, adultery, heartbreak, and even deeper darker secrets that you pray you don't want anyone to find out about have all kept you bound.

Perhaps you feel, unworthy, perhaps you believe that God doesn't know who you are. While the past cannot be changed, it can be erased and don't let anyone tell you otherwise. What has happened is just what happened, it does not matter at this point on the why it happened. Do you know how much energy and power you're giving away by trying to figure out why me? Do you know how much time is being wasted?

More than you can imagine. You're losing your grandest opportunity to excel. It is you who is keeping you down. The question you should be asking yourself as opposed to why me is what am I going to do about it? What can you do about it? I tell you this, the only thing you can do about it, is to change the way it makes you feel. If it makes you feel sad, immediately find something, anything that makes you feel good. Many people use the excuse that you cannot feel good about something that makes you feel bad. However, if you allow yourself to believe that, then that is exactly what will happen. You will remain feeling bad. But now how good is that going to feel? Wouldn't you rather feel good regardless of what has happened to you? Or are you content with allowing yourself to be the victim till you die in hopes that this heaven will give you peace. I tell you this, your peace is here, your peace is now, your peace is in the very next breath you take. If you allow it. The past has already happened. Say it aloud; The past has already happened. You're still standing, you're still breathing and what happens now is on you. The Creator only delivers what your vibrations sends out. What are you sending out dear friend? Are you sending out vibrations of love and peace and forgiveness and abundance or are you sending out vibrations of hate, resentment, revenge, pity, and jealousy? Today is the day to regenerate yourself and pay attention to your feelings. For these feelings send a greater message as to what you will receive from this moment on.

ACTION STEP

While knowledge is power, it's nothing if it's not applied.

So, let's apply an action step for what we just learned.

QUOTES TO CONSIDER:

Thoughts become things. Such as a man think so is, he. To

find yourself, think for yourself,

Misery is almost always the result of thinking.

What we think, we become.

What are you thinking right now?

 How is it making you feel?

List three thoughts of a time in your life that had you

laughing so hard you couldn't stop. A time where you felt

good. List those thoughts and feelings below.

STOP

Accountability

Do you believe this bad relationship is your entire fault? Are you on a job that pays you far from the value of the work you do? Do you have an issue finding a job? Do you even want a job, or do you want your own business? Regardless of what response you can relate to above, in the end, you were and are always in control of the outcome of these scenarios. This statement is not to make you angry, but to get you to understand you are accountable for what you allow others to do as well as your reactions to them. It's the action step you take after the fact that determines how far the rabbit hole will go. For example, you have a bank account that always seems to go into overdraft. You make a good salary, but you can't understand why you're always in the minus. How could this happen you ask yourself and you might even blame your spouse for pressuring you to do things that are beyond your financial capability at the time. You might even blame the bank for not taking money out when you spent it, that by the time they applied it, you had not funds to cover it. Well, who is it accountable for making sure you don't overspend? You are. If you have only $500 in the bank and you swipe your card, it doesn't matter when it's applied, you know you have only $500 available, thus any overspend is on you and the bank will be more than happy to oblige you since that is how they make money as well. Understand that you cannot fix a problem till you understand the source of where it's coming from. It may come from places beyond your control, but it's your responsibility to be aware, to be "present" always, regarding all things. To live any other way is a life lived irresponsibly, which in turns will take away your peace.

Action Steps

Using the journal provided below, take a moment to be honest with yourself once again and write down where you see yourself adding to your current negative circumstances.

Be honest, be accountable.

Make a list of all the things you are good at.

Don't sell yourself short. Take a deep honest look.

STOP Now make a list of the things you are passionate about. What is it that gets you excited when you?

Do it?

Finding Your Gifts

It is not expected of you to sit on the couch and play daydream all day long to keep your goals alive. You have work to do. Research that "thing" that is your goal. How can you prosper from it? What tools do you need?

Do you need more education to continue it? Etc.
You must make sure you do everything "you" can to get the ball moving. When you have reached a point that there is nothing left to do. Simply stop. This is where manifestation begins. A process is still going on.

Continue that "feeling" Change your circle of associates. Everything you do, speak of, breath and taste should be in your field of desire.
Educate your spirit. Why? Because it's a proven fact that when we don't see our works unfold, we get discourage

and begin with old habits that draw us far from our goal without even realizing it. Then we simply give up. Even worst, we use that old excuse "maybe it wasn't for me" It is always for you. But you must be the effect not the cause.

Don't wait for the opportunity, create it. Be the reason things happen, be the source of all good that comes to you. Be the master of your fate, through your knowing.

Knowing of your goals, knowing of the feeling it will give, knowing of the source. You. You are the effect. Repeat, I am the effect, I create the things in my life that I desire. I don't wait for opportunity, I don't wait till I have money, I don't wait, I act. I am the source.

In the words of the great philosopher Aristotle, Humans are what they repeatedly do; thus, excellence is not an act, it's a habit.

ACTION STEP

What gift did you uncover? Research to find out how you

monetize from it and put it to work for

you.

My gift & how I can make money from it.

STOP

Think Abundance

Now that you have a better understanding of how powerful you are and how much value you have, let's get into abundance. For what good would power and value be to a woman with no means to eat, drink and be merry?

For that is the goal. Don't make the huge mistake of allowing the ones behind the pulpit lead you to believe that The Creator wants you to be this broken life source, while he who stands behind the pulpit gets rich off your sweat and tears.

There are laws of the universe that once again have been hidden from you. If you have ever thought for a moment that The Creator set it up to allow the wicked to gain and the good to live in poverty, that only shows you just how disconnected you are from the lessons of the Creator. Did he not say you were the head not the tail? The only reason you have become the tail is because the head found out the laws of wealth and became selfish with it. Believing there would not be enough for everyone, most of all the wealthy crave power, and if you remember what we learned in the beginning of this book, the definition of power is the ability to influence people and circumstances. You now hold that same knowledge they had to become wealthy.

Whether you utilize it is solely on you. The definition of wealth is the abundance health, valuable possessions, or money.

Chapter 9 Action Steps

This next action step should be fun. It's time to create a mental image of how life would be if you had abundance. If money was not an issue.

Go online and search sites like, millionaire lifestyles, wealthy living, etc., go to car dealerships and sit in the car of your choice, the one that your heart desires but your pockets don't cooperate. Don't tell the dealer, you're just looking, tell him, you're comparing. Don't let him force you into doing any paperwork, ask for a test drive. Take the feeling that comes with driving this dream car and keep it in your memory bank. Dress your best and go visit upscale shops and browse, let the feeling of lack leave

your mind and the feeling of abundance seep in. Embrace it.

While this may seem crazy, you are creating a new vibration, you aren't doing some vision board, you're physically creating one. You are generating your thoughts become things moment. All you need to do now is

"believe" and keep the "emotion" of positivity flowing. Now, what is it that you desire? Think about it before you write it down and observe what

"feeling" it's giving you inside. Write it down, keep it

close, keep it to yourself, read it serval times a day.

We start by saying "I will "have never can't,

(the word can't confirm impossible) (the word will confirm

in the   process of)

I WILL HAVE

Freedom is the goal; money is a prerequisite of
that goal.

Many millionaires will tell you they started off broke. And
that is certainly true. What they won't tell you, but I will, is
that taking a financial inventory of your life is a necessity
to acquire wealth. How on earth can you achieve financial
freedom if you don't know exactly what you need. Many
people throw a magic number in the air like
"If only I had a million dollars" you'd be surprised at how
fast a million dollars can go. If you lack financial
discipline and you receive a million dollars, you will end up
going broke. Extremely fast.
The next step is to take a financial inventory of what you
owe and what you'd like to do if money wasn't an issue.
This way, your goal is having a starting point. The
principal of "Thoughts becomes things" play a big part
here. For example, if you find yourself saying I'm broke,

you're not only confirming, but declaring it, and since such as a man thinketh so is he, then Wolla! You might not have started it, but your surely making being broke a part of your life.   If you say," I just enough to pay my bills", then wolla! Once again, you got paid, you paid the bills, now there is nothing left. You are keeping a vibration that generates lack.

Change your thinking change your life.

ACTION STEP

This is the part where you might lose your enthusiasm, but hold on, change is coming.

For this exercise, you are to write down everyone you owe. Pull your credit report which is free by the way at www.freeannualcreditreport.com. Don't get discourage, but make a list of what your debt is, what you would like to do if money were not an issue, and how much does it cost you to run your everyday life. Add the debt and the expenses, multiply the total by twelve. This answer is what you need to have handy during the year. This just a starting point, you can have anything you desire, but you need a starting point.

MY FINANCIAL BLUEPRINT AS OF

(ENTER DATE)

ACQUIRING SUCESS

To make your goal to be wealthy is the worst goal you can ever wish for. Why?

Because to "want" already lays down the platform of lack. You are already affirming you don't have it when you do. Even worse, when you think that way, the goal has already been met. You wanted. Yes, you want, now what? Before you get all stubborn and angry at that statement, understand that the fact that you don't "believe" doesn't make it not so. Your goal should begin with "I WILL have" Whatever you would like to have, ask yourself, what would it feel like if you had it already. Would you be excited? Would you feel chills going down your back? Would you go shopping for that new car or house or both? These things are the things you should be focusing on the moment you understand what your goal is.

Now, go, window shop, (as instructed earlier) picture in

your mind with all that excitement what your new home would look like, where it would be, what kind of furniture you would have. A swimming pool perhaps. Go all in with it. Write out a check payable to yourself, with a date, an amount and put it somewhere you can see daily. The action step here is to keep the experience of the outcome of your goal

alive.

ACTION STEP:

How I felt as I window shopped to create a positive internal feeling.

Conclusion

In conclusion, let us be clear that none of the authors or writers are proposing that transforming your emotions and controlling your words and thoughts are a simple recipe for the perfect moment. We are saying, however, that it is the solution and most imperative tool in order for you to be an active co-creative while in the physical plane. We are saying that when you remember that we are all one, part of Universal Intelligence and not a separate unit, we are saying that everything in your path is the result of what you have focused on or the most, good, or not so good.

We are also saying that when you hold on to negative experiences, it creates negative emotions which creates negative prompters and those prompters set the stage for the next incident. When you focus on being present, and when you focus on being in control of your mind instead of the mind being in control of you, and even once you have learned to master your emotions in spite of what lies before you. In all these steps, can you become a positive active co-creator of your life?

Learning to say what we mean and mean what we say, should be carefully thought out before uttered, lest our moment be filled with chaos. We are all here to experience what we choose to experience, and it is not only what happens to us from our thoughts, actions, and words that create awesome manifestations, but in that, we should recognize the power we have been given through the ability to speak life into situations in our surroundings, in our communicates and the world we live so that, there can truly be a serene experience for all lives involved.

Let us remember to focus not just on material manifestations but that of our health. And why? You may wonder. Our health in its optimist state allows the possibility of longevity. In this longevity, comes more time to produce positive vibrations for humanity as a whole. We cannot help humanity if we cannot help ourselves. The power of three should be practiced not just once daily, but every time, you find thoughts approaching in the mind, emotions rising inwardly be it good or bad and every moment before words are formed from the lips.

Practicing speaking life into all things, from the smallest insect to the largest animal, from the plant that appears to be dying from lack of sun or water to the tallest tree that is being threatened to be cut down for man's selfish gain. These things are big in nature and serve a higher purpose, if you can learn to see the value in what is considered to be irrelevant, you will find it easier to modify, manage and master your thoughts, your words, and your emotions.

In final reflection, I hold myself accountable for ensuring my position as a Metaphysical Practitioner, to remember to think before I speak, hold tight my tongue in times of frustration, and make it my duty to change my direction of thinking so that my thoughts match my words and emotions in a way that serves humanity for the greater good. For what good are we if we continue to think as a singular unit or even a selfish one if we put ourselves so high in delight that we forget our brethren. Even as much as I and should all mankind, be mindful in thinking good things forth into this world. Using the power of loving thoughts, the power of positive words, and genuine feelings of love for every living breathing thing upon this planet. The power of three is my tool to make not only my life but the world around me a better place.

So yes, I call forth the Universe, The Force, Universal Intelligence, The Holy Spirit, and The Vortex, and into I pour positive emotions, positive words, and thoughts of love, peace, and joy for all mankind. I AM the captain of my ship and master of my fate and with such power, I use it to activate the power of three, My positive words, my loving emotions, and my thoughts for good. I say it is so, and so it is.

You have just read and applied several chapters worth of action steps that will change the way you see yourself, the world, you're thinking, your emotional vibrations, and if you are repeating them on a weekly basis, you are creating a new and powerful habit. Do not toss this book to the side once you're done. Read your notes,

Then re-read, and keep it to yourself. Allow yourself room for slip ups but get back up. When you understand how these things are transforming you into a Power thinker who applies logic and knows no limits you cannot be played, you will excel and if you add your own flavor of individualism, you are unstoppable.

You Are God's Greatest Masterpiece!! Now, go and change your world.

*Footnote: Understand that no matter what your spiritual beliefs are, the universal law is working whether you believe it or not. *
You are the greatest creation

Know it!

Live it!

Be it now!

Works Cited

Anderson, Uell S. *The Key to Power and Personal Peace.* Hermitage House; 1st edition (1954) e-book

Braden Gregg, *The Divine Matrix. New York NY. Hay House. 2007. Print*

Byrne, Rhonda, The Power. New York. Simon & Shulster Inc. 2010 c book

Gandhi, Mahatma quote: *http://www.lifepowertip.com/watchyourthoughts.html.* Web

Goddard Neville, *Feeling is The Secret. Watchmaker Publishing 2012. e-book*

Handlin Henry. *The Power of Thought.* Published August 21st, 2007, by Ancient Wisdom Publications *London UK 2008. e-book*

Hicks Abraham *Ask and It Is Given. Abraham-Hicks Publications 1997.e-book*

Jones, Daniel M. Becoming the Force. London. Watkins Publishing. 2017.Print

Lerner Kettler D. JS Emotions & Decisions: Annual Review of Psychology 2010 page 315-352. https://www.annualreviews.org/doi/full/10.1146/annurev-psych-0 10213-115043. Web

Metaphysics for Life. (www.metaphysics-for-life.com/thoughts-become-things.html). web

Murphy Joseph, Cosmic Energizer, Miracle Power of the Universe. West Nyack, NY. Parker Publishing 1974. Print

Peale, Norman Vincent The Power of Positive Thinking. New York NY Simon & Shulster 1952 Print

Shaw Andy, Mastering the Law of Attraction. Amazon Digital Kdp Print. 2014 e-book

Solomon RC. 1993, Passions, Emotions, and the Meaning of Life. New York, NY. Hackett Publishing Company, Inc. 1993. e-book

Notes. Affirmations & Thoughts

Made in the USA
Columbia, SC
19 October 2022